Eva's Adventures In Shadow-land

Mary Dummett Nauman

EVA'S ADVENTURES

IN

SHADOW-LAND.

" The Toad Woman stopped fanning and looked at her."

Frontispiece.]   Page 125.

EVA'S ADVENTURES

IN

SHADOW-LAND.

BY MARY D. NAUMAN,

AUTHOR OF "TWISTED THREADS," "THE GOLD THIMBLE," ETC.

WITH ILLUSTRATIONS.

PHILADELPHIA:
J. B. LIPPINCOTT & CO.
1872.

"... to the corner I am ..."

Page 84.

Eva's Adventures

IN

SHADOW-LAND.

Robinson

By MARY D. NAUMAN,

AUTHOR OF "TWISTED THREADS," "SIDNEY ELLIOTT," ETC.

WITH ILLUSTRATIONS.

PHILADELPHIA:
J. B. LIPPINCOTT & CO.
1872.

TO

MY FRIEND

E. W.

CONTENTS.

(vii)

EVA'S ADVENTURES

IN SHADOW-LAND.

CHAPTER I.

WHAT EVA SAW IN THE POND.

SHE had been reading fairy-tales, after her lessons were done, all the morning; and now that dinner was over, her father gone to his office, the baby asleep, and her mother sitting quietly sewing in the cool parlor, Eva thought that she would go down across the field to the old mill-pond; and sit in the grass, and make a fairy-tale for herself.

There was nothing that Eva liked better than to go and sit in the tall grass; grass so tall that when the child, in her white dress, looped on her plump white shoulders with blue ribbons, her bright golden curls brushed back from her fair brow, and

(9)

her blue eyes sparkling, sat down in it, you could not see her until you were near her, and then it was just as if you had found a picture of a little girl in a frame, or rather a nest of soft, green grass.

All through this tall, wavy grass, down to the very edge of the pond, grew many flowers,— violets, and buttercups, and dandelions, like little golden suns. And as Eva sat there in the grass, she filled her lap with the purple and yellow flowers; and all around her the bees buzzed as though they wished to light upon the flowers in her lap; on which, at last,—so quietly did she sit, —two black-and-golden butterflies alighted; while a great brown beetle, with long black feelers, climbed up a tall grass-stalk in front of her, which, bending slightly under his weight, swung to and fro in the gentle breeze which barely stirred Eva's golden curls; and the field-crickets chirped, and even a snail put his horns out of his shell to look at the little girl, sitting so quietly in the grass among the flowers, for Eva was gentle, and neither bee, nor butterfly, beetle, cricket, or snail were afraid of her. And this is what Eva called making a fairy-tale for herself.

But sitting so quietly and watching the insects, and hearing their low hum around her, at last made Eva feel drowsy; and she would have gone to sleep, as she often did, if all of a sudden there had not sounded, just at her feet, so that it startled her, a loud

Croak! croak!

But it frightened the two butterflies; for away they went, floating off on their black-and-golden wings; and the brown beetle was in so much of a hurry to run away that he tumbled off the grass-stalk on which he had been swinging, and as soon as he could regain his legs, crept, as fast as they could carry him, under a friendly mullein-leaf which grew near, and hid himself; and the crickets were silent; and the bees all flew away to their hive; and the snail drew himself and his horns into his house, so that he looked like nothing in the world but a shell; for when beetles, and but-terflies, and crickets, and bees, and snails hear this croak! croak! they know that it is time for them to get out of the way.

And when Eva looked down, there, just at her feet, sat a great green toad.

She gave him a little push with her foot to make him go away; but instead of that he only hopped the nearer, and again came—

Croak! croak!

He was entirely too near now for comfort, so the little girl jumped up, dropping all the flowers she had gathered; and as she stood still for a moment she thought that she heard the green toad say:

"Go to the pond! Go to the pond!"

It seemed so funny to Eva to hear a toad talk that she stood as still as a mouse looking at him; and as she looked at him, she heard him say again, as plain as possible:

"Go to the pond! Go to the pond!"

And then Eva did just exactly what either you or I would have done if we had heard a great green toad talking to us. She went slowly through the tall grass down to the very edge of the pond.

But instead of the fishes which used to swim about in the pretty clear water, and which would come to eat the crumbs of bread she always threw to them, and the funny, croaking frogs which used to jump and splash in the water, she saw nothing

but the same great green toad, which had hopped
down faster than she had walked, and which was
now sitting on a mossy stone near the bank. And
when Eva would have turned away he croaked
again:

"Stay by the pond! Stay by the pond!"

And whether Eva wished it or not, she stood by
the pond—for she really could not help it—and
looked. And it seemed to her that the sky grew
dark and the water black, as it always does before
a rain; and then the child grew frightened, and
would have run away, but that just then, in the
very blackest part of the pond, she saw shining
and looking up at her a little round full moon,
with a face in it; and it seemed to her, strange
though you may think it, that the eyes of the face
in the moon winked at her; and then it was gone.

And again Eva would have left the pond, but
the green toad, which she thought had suddenly
grown larger, croaked more loudly:

"Stay by the pond! Stay by the pond!"

And Eva obeyed, as indeed she could not help
doing; and then again, in the pond, there came
and went the little moon-face, only that this time
it was larger, and the eyes winked longer.

B

For the third time the child would have turned away, frightened at all these strange doings in the pond; but for the third time the green toad, larger than ever, croaked :

"Stay by the pond !   Stay by the pond !"

So, for the third time, Eva looked at the pond ; and there, for the third time, was the shining moon-face, as large now as a real full moon, though, when Eva looked up, there was no moon shining in the sky to be reflected in the pond ; and then the eyes in the moon-face looked harder at her, and the toad winked at her; and then the toad was the moon and the moon was the toad, and both seemed to change places with each other ; and at last both of them shone and winked so that Eva could not tell them apart; and before she knew what she was doing she lay down quietly in the tall grass, and the moon in the pond and the green toad winked at her until she fell asleep.

Then the moon-eyes closed and the shining face faded ; and the green toad slipped quietly off his stone into the water; and still Eva slept soundly.

And that was what Eva saw in the pond.

CHAPTER II.

EVA'S FIRST ADVENTURE.

OW long she lay there asleep the child did not know. It might only have been for a few minutes; it might have been for hours. Yet, when she did awake, and think it was time for her to go home, she did not understand where she could be. The place seemed the same, yet not the same,—as though some wonderful change had come over it during her sleep. There was the pond, to be sure, but was it the same pond? Tall trees grew round it, yet their branches were bare and leafless. A little brook ran into the pond, which she was sure that she never had seen there before. Was she still asleep? No. She was wide awake. She sprang to her feet and looked around. The green toad was gone, so was the moon-face; her father's house was nowhere to be seen; there was no sun, but it was not dark, for a light seemed to come from the earth, and yet the earth itself did not shine; mountains rose in the distance; but, strangest of all, these mountains sometimes bore one shape, sometimes another; at times they were like great crouching beasts, then again like castles or palaces, then, as you looked, they were mountains again. Strange shadows passed over the pond, stranger shapes flitted among the trees.

Eva did not know how the change had been made, still less did she guess that she was now in Shadow-Land.

Yet it was all so singular that, as she looked upon the changing mountain forms, and the quaint shadows, a sudden longing came over her, with a desire to go home, and she turned away from the pond. And as she did so, a little fragrant purple violet, the last that was left of all the flowers which she had gathered, and which had been tangled in her curls, fell to the ground, melting into fragrance as it did so; and as it fell, there passed from Eva's mind all recollection of father, mother, home, and the little brother cooing in his cradle: the changing mountain forms seemed strange no longer; she forgot to wonder at the singular earth-light, and at the absence of the sun; and noticing for the first time that she was standing in a little path which ran along the pond, and then followed the course of the little brook, whose waters seemed singing the words, "Follow, follow me!" Eva wondered no longer, but first stooping to pick up a little stick, in shape like a boy's cane, with a knob at one end, just like a roughly carved head, and which was lying just at her feet, she walked along the little path, which seemed made expressly for her to walk in.

She walked on and on, as she thought, for hours, yet there came neither sunset nor moon-rise, and there were no stars in the sky, which seemed nearer the earth than she had ever seen it before. There were clouds, to be sure, of shapes as strange as those of the mountains, which passed and repassed each other, although there was no wind to move them. Everything was silent. Even the trees, swaying, as they did, to and fro, moved noiselessly; the only sound, save Eva's light steps, which broke the stillness was the silvery ripple of the brook, which kept company with the path Eva trod, and whose waters murmured, gently, "Follow, follow me!"

And Eva followed the murmuring brook, which seemed to her like a pleasant companion in this silent land, where, even as there was no sound, there was no sign of life; nothing like the real world which the child had left, and of which, with the fall of the little violet from her curls, she had lost all recollection; even as though that world had never existed for her. Once or twice, as she went on, holding her little stick in her hand, she imagined that she saw child-figures beckoning to her; but, upon going up to them, she always found that either a rock, or a low, leafless shrub, or else a rising wreath of mist, had deceived her.

Yet, though she was alone, with no one near her, not even a bird to flit merrily from tree to tree, nor an insect to buzz across her path, Eva felt and knew no fear, and not for a moment did she care that she was alone. The silvery ripple of the little brook, along which her path lay, sounded like a pleasant voice in her ears; when thirsty, she drank of its waters, which seemed to serve alike as food and drink; when tired, she would lie fearlessly down upon its grassy margin, and sleep, as she would imagine, only for a few minutes, for there would be no change in the strange sky nor in the earth-light when she would awake from what it had been when she lay down; and yet in reality she would sleep as long as she would have done in her little bed at home.

· For two whole days, which yet seemed as only a few hours, the child followed the brook. During this time she had felt no desire to leave the path; she had unhesitatingly obeyed the rippling voice of the brook, which seemed to say, "Follow, follow me!" But now there was a change: the water, at times, encroached upon the path, and rocks obstructed the current, around which little waves broke and dashed, while strange little flames, which yet did not burn, and gave no heat, started from the waves, dancing on them; and misty shapes, more definite than those she had first seen, beckoned to her to come to them. Now, Eva felt an irresistible longing to leave the brook, and wander away; far, far into the deep forest, away from the dancing flames and the beckoning shapes.

And once or twice she did leave the path, and turn her back upon the brook. But every time that she stepped off the beaten track, faint though it was, her feet grew heavy, and clung to the earth, so that she could scarcely move; and the waves of the brook leaped higher and higher; and the dancing flames grew brighter; and the silvery voice, louder and clearer than ever, would call, "Follow, follow me!" till the child was always glad to return to the path, and then once again the way would grow easy to her feet, and the water would resume its former tranquillity.

On, on she went, still following the course of the brook. But at last a new sound mingled, though but faintly, with its musical ripple,—the distant voice of falling waters. And when first this new tone reached Eva's ears, a few signs of life began to show themselves,—a sad-colored moth flitted lazily across the path into the forest, —a slow-crawling worm or hairy caterpillar hid itself under a stone as Eva passed,—the bright eyes of a mouse would peep out at her from under the shelter of a leaf, or else a toad would leap hastily from the path into the waters of the brook.

Still Eva walked onward, more eagerly than ever, for though the "Follow, follow me!" of the brook was now silent, she heard the voice of the other waters, and at every turn in the path she looked forward eagerly for the little joyous cascade she expected to see. For it she looked, yet in vain: though the sound of the waters grew louder, she saw nothing, till at last a sudden gleam of golden light, from a long opening in the forest, fell across the now placid waters of the brook; and Eva looked up to see, far away in this opening, a fountain playing in clouds of golden spray, amid which danced sparkles of light; and the path, parting abruptly from the brook which it had followed so long, led down the opening in the forest directly to this play of waters, whose voice Eva had heard and followed.

And as she turned away from the little brook, whose course and her own had so long been the same, it seemed to her that even the silvery ripple of its waters died away into silence ; and, looking back once more, after she had taken a few steps, upon the way by which she had come, lo ! the brook and its waters had wholly disappeared, and an impenetrable forest had already closed up the path behind her.

CHAPTER III.

THE GIFT OF THE FOUNTAIN.

I HAVE said that Eva wondered at nothing which came to pass in this land through which she was wandering; nothing surprised her, but the most singular occurrences appeared natural; and so it did not seem at all strange to her that the path and the brook should be swallowed up, as it were, by the dark, hungry, impenetrable forest; and it was almost with a feeling of pleasure at the change that after the one hurried glance she gave to the path by which she had come, and which was now no longer to be seen, that she went, still holding the little stick in her hand, up the opening between the trees to the beautiful fountain.

And, as she drew near, the bright waters of the fountain played higher and higher, and sparkled and glistened in golden beauty ; and rainbows of many colors surrounded it, so that Eva longed to dip her hands in its joyous flow, while the waters as they fell tinkled merrily like silvery fairy bells ; and she came nearer and nearer, thinking she had never heard such sweet music as this water made, till she was within a few feet of the fountain.

But when there she paused. For, out of the earth,—all round and even under the dropping spray and the falling waters,—sprang myriads of little rainbow-colored flames, which danced to and fro among and under the water-drops,—like a circle of tiny, fiery sentinels, guarding the fountain. And Eva, afraid to cross this circle of flames, for which she was unprepared, would not have ventured nearer, but that at this very moment the little stick which she held turned in her hand, and pointed downward ; and then Eva saw that it pointed to a little path, like that by which she had come, which ran around the fountain ; and the child followed the path, until she had walked once, twice, thrice, around the playing waters, and yet, though she looked for it, found no spot where the little flame-sentinels, like faithful soldiers on duty, would permit her to pass. And then she would have turned away from the beautiful water,—her foot, indeed, had left the path,—when she heard a voice, even sweeter and more silvery than the voice of the brook, coming from the very midst of the fountain, and saying:

> "Eva! Eva! have no fear,
> To the fountain's brink come near."

And hearing these words, Eva stood still in surprise, yet without obeying them. But, after a moment's pause, the voice repeated the words.

Then, for the first time since her wanderings had begun, Eva spoke, and her voice sounded strange in her own ears, low though it was:

"How can I cross the fire?"

A little, low, melodious laugh, like that of a merry child, answered her; and when Eva looked to see whence it came, she saw that the little knot upon the end of her cane was a real head, that the lips were laughing, and that from the queer eyes came two funny little blue flames; and as

C

Eva looked at it, very much tempted to throw it away, the head laughed again, and then the lips parted and said :

> " Flames, like these, of shadow birth,
>   May not harm a child of earth."

Then the voice was silent. But a thousand rainbow-colored bubbles glowed at once all over the waters of the fountain ; and on each bubble there stood and danced a tiny elf, clad in bright colors ; shapes so light and airy that their frail supports never failed them ; and the tiny flames grew brighter, and then, as Eva still hesitated, fearing yet to cross them, the lips of the little head spoke once more :

> " 'Neath thy step they will expire—
>   Fear not, Eva ; cross the fire."

Hearing this, Eva stepped forward. As she did so, the little stick dropped or slipped from her hand, and, rolling into the fountain, disappeared in its waters ; and at every step she took she saw that the little flames died away, as the voice had said, under her feet ; till, when she reached the fountain's brink, they were all gone, and no trace of them was left. As she looked at the waters, they seemed to become solid, and shape themselves into an image carved as it were out of pure, shining gold, yet glowing with many colors; and then, slowly, slowly, with a sound like distant music, the beautiful, wonderful thing began to sink into the earth; and Eva, her tiny hands clasped, her fair cheeks flushed, her soft blue eyes sparkling, stood in silence and looked. And just as the magic fountain, which, when the child first came up to it, had been so high that its waters played far above her head, had sunk so low that Eva, had she wished, might have laid her hand upon its summit, she saw, cradled as it were, on the very crest of what had been the golden water, a tiny figure; not like one of the elves which had danced on the rainbow-bubbles, but like a sleeping child, which Eva thought, at first, was only a doll lying there, in its green-and-scarlet velvet dress; and for a moment the slow, descending motion of the fountain stopped, and Eva heard these words, in the same voice which had spoken before through the lips of the little head, though this time it came from the fountain:

"Take it, Eva, 'tis thy fate,
See, for thee the waters wait."

Obedient to the voice, the child stretched forth her hand, and as her slight fingers closed upon the little, motionless form, a bright and dazzling crimson light seemed to flash everywhere, and the water, losing its solidity, began once more to gleam and sparkle, and to sink again into the earth; and in another moment it was gone, and in the place where the fountain had played there was now a bed of soft, green moss, through and around which was twined a vine, whose leaves were mingled with clusters of bright scarlet berries. Then for the first time she missed her little stick; and she looked for it, but it was nowhere to be found.

And then the sky grew dark, as the glorious crimson light slowly faded away, and one by one stars peeped out from the sky; and Eva, still clasping the little figure which had come so strangely to her, to her heart, lay down quietly upon the soft, green moss, which seemed to have sprung up there expressly as a bed for her, and before many minutes had passed she was asleep.

But while she slept, there hovered over her two fair white forms, who looked at her and smiled, and then one of them whispered to the other, in the silvery voice of the brook :

" The worst is over."

" No," the other replied. " Although the boy is safe, for a time, in the hands of his protector, his punishment is not yet over. Love must teach him obedience,—that alone can appease and work out the will of Fate."

" And we can do no more for him !"

" We can only wait, and hope."

A moment later, and the two bright forms were gone. And, watched by the twinkling stars, lulled by the low murmur of the gentle breeze playing among the trees of the great forest, the fair child slept, holding clasped to her innocent breast the helpless figure which had come to her as the gift of the fountain.

CHAPTER IV.

THE FIRST MOONRISE.

BUT sleep does not last forever, and after a time Eva awoke. And when she first sat up, and looked around her, she could not understand, for a moment, how it could be that everything was so changed; why the brook should be gone, and its voice silenced; the path no more to be seen; and how she should be sitting on this soft bed of velvety-green moss, with the little figure lying in her lap. Then, all at once, she remembered all that had happened the day before, — and as she thought it over, like a pleasant, yet indistinct dream, she recalled the two fair forms which had hovered over her sleep, —faintly conscious of their presence, though unaware of the words which they had spoken. Whether they were real, or only a dream, Eva did not know; she only recalled them mistily; for, in this strange, silent land, through which she was wandering, she never knew what was real or what unreal,—it was all alike to her.

And as nothing that happened astonished her, so never for one moment did her thoughts go back to the father and mother she had left, or to the little baby-brother cooing in his cradle. It was as though they never had existed, so completely were they forgotten. The Present, such as it was, had effaced all memory of that Past.

Sitting on her soft, mossy bed, still holding in her little hands the motionless little figure which the fountain had left her, and which, Eva knew,—though how she knew it she could not tell,—was something to be cared for and guarded, as being more helpless than herself. Eva thought over all the adventures of the day before, and while she wondered what would come next, she wished she could once more hear the pleasant murmur of the brook which had guided her, for what purpose she knew not, to this spot.

Only a few moments had passed since the child awoke, when a low, musical chime rang through

the forest.   It died away and then returned ; and
then came again and again, in tones so marvel-
lously sweet that Eva, who had just taken the
little figure into her hands, dropped him into her
lap, and pushed her long golden curls away from
her face, the better to listen to the melody.

Once more it came, and once more died away
into silence.   And then there was a low, rushing
sound, and, far in the distance, Eva saw arise, as it
were from out of the earth, among the trees, the
tiny silver crescent of a young new moon,—and as
she looked at it, it rose higher and higher, and
faster and faster, till it reached, in a few minutes,
the very centre of the sky, the child's blue eyes
still following it ; and when once there it paused,
and floated among the strange, gleaming clouds,
which surrounded it, like a little shining boat.

With a sudden impulse Eva bent down and
kissed the little figure lying in her lap ; and then
she looked up at the crescent of the moon, as
upon the face of an old friend ; and she would
have sat there longer watching it, but that all at
once a little, weak voice said :

"I am awake again, and there is my home."

"—taking off the plumed hat which he wore, he made her a very low bow."

Then there came a hurried exclamation of surprise, and Eva looked down from the moon's crescent to see that the little figure which she had taken from the crest of the fountain had suddenly, as it were, been gifted by her kiss, with life, motion, and speech, and that he was now standing in her lap, evidently as much astonished at seeing her as she was at the change which had come over him.

But their mutual surprise did not last; for the little mannikin began to laugh as Eva's blue eyes grew larger and rounder, and when at last she asked, "Who are you?" he put his head to one side, in the most comical manner, and, taking off the plumed cap which he wore, he made her a very low bow.

"I know now who you are," he said. "You are Eva, and you will have to take care of me,—that is all you were sent here for."

Eva laughed. "Suppose I should not want to take care of such a little thing as you are?"

"You will not have any choice in the matter,—you cannot help yourself."

"Why?"

"Because THEY have said it."

"I may not choose to do it."

"What is the use of talking," the boy went on, "when you know that you will?"

And such were the answers that he persisted in giving to all her inquiries.

"You said you knew who I was," Eva went on; "but how did you know it?"

"THEY told me."

"Who are THEY?"

"THEY led you here to me, and for me. You must not ask so many questions."

"May I not even ask your name?"

"You ought to know that without my telling you. But, as you don't, I will answer you. It is Aster."

"Aster? Aster?" Eva slowly repeated; "it seems to me that I have heard that name before."

"You never did," was the somewhat sullen answer; "for no one but myself has any right to it."

"Yet I am very sure that I have heard it before, at——"

"Hush! hush! You must never say that here," said the miniature boy, climbing up on Eva's shoulder, and laying his hand upon her lips. "You know as well as I do that you never heard my name before."

"I thought I had," Eva said, looking lovingly at the little figure nestling among her golden curls; "but I now know that I never did. Still, I would like to know who you are. Are you a fairy?"

"I am not a fairy, but you are all mine," Aster said, gayly. "But you must be careful with me, and never lose me, or else——"

"What?"

"I do not know. THEY are watching us."

Who "THEY" were, Eva could not induce him to say. For even when he did try to explain, his words were all so confused that Eva could not understand at all what he meant, although he seemed to speak plainly; and the only thing that she could really learn from him was this,—that she must not ask questions, and that THEY were THEY.

Which is all very strange to us; but it appears that Eva was at last satisfied, because Aster seemed to think that she should understand it just as he did, and that nothing further need, consequently, be said on the subject.

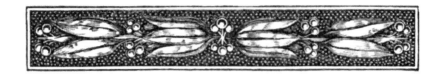

CHAPTER V.

WHAT ASTER WAS.

FOR several days the two, Eva and Aster, wandered through the forest with no object in view, and returned every evening to rest upon the soft, mossy bed which now covered the place where the golden fountain had once played. The scarlet berries of the vine surrounding it gave them food. The young moon, floating in the sky, gave them light; for while she shone, it was their day; when, suddenly as she arose, she would drop from the centre of the sky, then came their night; and the hours of her absence were spent in sleep.

So, at stated intervals, the moon sprang suddenly from the earth, shone there, replacing the faint earth-light which, during her absence, had guided Eva, and which still shone when she was not to be seen; then, after her hours were over, she as suddenly descended; and her rising and her setting were alike accompanied by the same weird music which had heralded her first coming, though its notes were fainter than those which had hailed the rising of the young new moon.

But every time that the moon returned it seemed to Eva that she grew brighter and larger, and that she shed more light upon the earth. And as the light grew brighter, pale white flowers began here and there to bloom, flowers which drooped and closed their petals as soon as the moon fell from the sky; flowers which, as Eva thought, murmured a low song as she passed them, yet a song whose words she never could distinguish. And at last she noticed that, as the silver crescent of the moon broadened, the slight form of Aster seemed to grow and to expand, so that he was no longer the tiny doll-like figure which she had taken from the fountain's crest, but more like a boy of four years old.

Yet this change, although it was singular, was only a source of pleasure to the child. It gave her a companion, not merely a plaything, for until now she had looked upon Aster in that light,—

D

something which, though it could talk, walk,
sleep, and eat, was only a new toy, to be taken care
of and prized as such. She never had looked
upon Aster otherwise.

At last, when the moon had reached her first
quarter, and the two, enjoying her pure light, sat
on their mossy bed, Eva asked the boy the same
question she had asked him the day her first kiss
had awakened him:

"Tell me who yóu are."

"I am Aster."

"I know that," Eva said, laying her hand on
the boy's shoulder; "but that is only your name."

"I shall be as large as you are, soon," Aster
said, raising his star-like eyes to the moon as he
spoke. "When she is round, I shall be as tall as
you are, Eva."

Eva laughed. "How do you know?"

"It will be; because it must be."

"You are Aster," Eva said, slowly, "and I
know how you came to me; but why did you
come?"

"You will know then."

"When?"

"When the moon is round."

"Why not now?"

"THEY will not let you."

And with this answer Eva was forced to be content. But every day they would stand side by side, and every day Aster grew taller and taller; and every day the moon grew broader and brighter.

At last she rose, a round, perfect orb, to her station in the sky; and as Eva, awakened by the loud music which told of her coming, sat up to see and wonder at the bright light she cast, Aster came quietly behind her, and, laying his hands on her shoulders, said:

"Look at me, Eva. The day has come, and I am as tall as you are."

Eva sprang to her feet. As she did so, Aster put his arm around her, and she saw that there was now no difference in their height,—they were exactly the same size. And, strange to say, his clothes had grown with him, and their rich, soft velvet fitted him now as perfectly as it had done when Eva first took him, small and helpless, from the crest of the golden fountain.

"I can tell you now who I am," the beautiful

boy said, "for to-day THEY cannot silence me; this one day when I can be my own self again. You ought to know, Eva, without my telling you, and you would know, if you were like me; but you are not as I am."

"Why not?" Eva asked, in surprise.

"Because you are only a little earth-maiden."

Eva laughed. "What is that?" She had wholly, as we know, forgotten the past.

"I cannot tell you," Aster said, slowly. "I only know what THEY have told me about you."

"And that?"

"I do not know. But you are not like me, Eva. We are very different. Look at your dress, and then at mine."

In truth, every here and there upon the rich velvet of Aster's dress were soils and stains, while not a spot discolored the pure white Eva wore.

"Now do you see?" Aster asked. "You know that we are in Shadow-Land, and it can only affect things which are like itself; it cannot harm you or deceive you."

"Do you belong here?"

"No," Aster said. "I came from there,"

pointing to the round full moon above their heads. "I wish I was there again."

"Why don't you go back, then?"

"I can't, unless you help me. THEY who sent me here say so."

"Why did they send you here?"

"Because up there," pointing to the moon, "I lost my flower, and everything which is lost there falls into Shadow-Land, as everything which is lost in Fairy-Land falls into the Enchanted River; and so they sent me here to find it again, because a prince cannot live there without his flower; and I cannot find it unless you help me. Now you know who I am, Eva,—the moon-prince, Aster."

"Then must I say Prince Aster?"

"No; to you I am only Aster. And I know that it will be hard for you to find the flower, for I cannot help you, or tell you what it is like. I know that the Green Frog has hidden it, and you are the only person who can help me to find it, and then you must give it to me. THEY say we shall have trouble."

"But we will find it at last?"

"When my punishment for losing it is over. To-morrow we must leave this place, for after this moon the moss will be gone."

"You know where to go, then?"

"No; I can only follow you. I have no power here; you will have to take care of me."

And then Aster began to sing, and this was the song which he sung:

> Till my flower bloom again,
> We may seek, yet seek in vain.
> Till 'tis plucked by Eva's hand,
> We must roam through Shadow-Land.
>
> Only this does Aster know,
> Through hard trials he must go;
> Eva's hand must guide him on
> Till his flower again be won.
>
> She must wander far and near,
> Led by songs he may not hear;
> Should she lose me from her hand,
> Worse my fate in Shadow-Land.

Then Aster threw himself down on the soft moss at Eva's feet. But when she asked him where he had learned the words of his song, he

could not tell her. Just then a cloud came over
the face of the moon, hiding her from their sight;
and as the darkness came over everything, only
leaving for a moment the pale earth-light, it
seemed to Eva that there were faces looking at
her, peeping from behind every tree; and then
a light breeze sprang up, just moving the flowers,
and from the bell of one of them seemed to come
these words, all in verse, for in Fairy-Land and in
Shadow-Land people seldom speak in plain prose
as we do :

> O'er this spot do THEY have power,
> Not here groweth Aster's flower.
> Wander, Eva, wander on
> Till thy hand the prize hath won.

Then the breeze died away, and the voice was
silent; and Eva saw that Aster was asleep, and,
frightened at the faces which made grimaces and
mocked at her, more angrily, she thought, on ac-
count of the warning the flower had sung, she
touched him to awaken him; and as she did so
the cloud passed from the face of the moon, and
as once more her pure, clear light returned,
the ugly, threatening faces vanished, and Aster

awoke.   But when Eva tried to tell him of what she had seen and heard during his short sleep, she could only say these words:

> Moss shall harden into stone,
>> Faces mock you o'er the sand;
>> Leading Aster by the hand,
> From this spot ye must be gone.

Then Aster laughed, because Eva declared that these were not the words which the flower had spoken; yet every time that she tried to recollect and repeat them, she could only say the same thing over.   Then she began to try and tell him about the faces, and when she began to speak of them, suddenly the full moon sank from the sky, and all was dark; and then a strange drowsiness came over the children, and Eva and Aster, nestled in each other's arms, lay down to sleep upon the soft, green moss, knowing that with the next moonrise they must go forth in search of Aster's lost flower.

CHAPTER VI.

THE BEGINNING OF THE SEARCH.

WHEN the two children, after their sleep, awoke to see the moon rise to her station in the sky, they were not surprised to find that her fair, round proportions were already changed. But when Eva turned to Aster, she saw that he, too, was smaller than when they had lain down to rest; and she knew at once, almost as if she had been told, that the Moon-Prince would in future wax and wane as did the orb from which he had been banished; that this was part of his punishment; and now she understood why it was that Aster had said she would have to take care of him. But as she stood, thinking of this, Aster suddenly touched her hand, and directly over the mossy bed on which they had

(45)

slept, and which had never been crushed by their weight, but was always fresh, Eva saw again the mocking faces which had disturbed her the night before; but only for a moment, and then they were gone. And even as she looked, she saw that the soft green moss began to shrivel, dry up, and crumble away, as though in a fire; and a moment later it was all gone, and in its place was a heap of rough sand and stone, instead of the velvety moss and the vine with its scarlet berries.

"The faces have done it," Eva said, clasping Aster's hand tightly, as she watched the rapid change.

"The faces!" Aster said, scornfully. "Eva, you are dreaming; there were no faces there."

"I saw them," Eva began; but Aster interrupted her.

"I tell you, Eva, you saw no faces, there was nothing there. I told you that the moss would be gone the next time that the moon rose; and you see I told you the truth. We must leave this place."

"Where shall we go?"

"I don't know. We cannot stay here. What did the flower say to you, Eva?

> When soft moss shall change to stone,
> From this spot ye must be gone."

Even as Aster spoke, Eva saw a faint little path at her feet, like that which she had first followed. Looking back, wishing it might lead her again to the pleasant little brook, and that she might return to it, instead of going on into the forest, she saw that the sand and stone had grown into a huge wall, or rather a mound, over which she never could have climbed, and which would prevent her return. As if Aster had read her thoughts, he said to her,—

"There is no going back, Eva; we can only go forward."

Aster's words were true. The wall of stone, which a few moments had been enough to build up behind them, seemed to come closer and closer, as though to shut them out from the place where they had been; and, clasping Aster's hand tightly, Eva and the boy walked slowly on, in the little path which lay before them.

For days the two went on, walking while the
moon shone, and sleeping when her light was hid.
At each moonrise they were awakened by the
strains of music, which, as the moon waned, grew
sadder and more mournful; while that accom-
panying her setting became at last a low, sad
moaning, and each day she grew smaller, and,
in sympathy with her, Aster seemed to dwindle
and wane, and he became more and more helpless, till at last, when the moon was reduced to a
thin crescent, the little prince was once more as
small as he was when Eva first received him.

Yet, through all these changes, the two went
slowly on through the dark forest, which opened
on either side of the path to let them pass, and
closed again behind them. Were they thirsty,
they were sure to find some tiny spring, issuing
as at a wish from the earth; were they hungry,
some wild fruit or berry was always to be found.
But not once did Eva leave the path. What it
was that kept her in it, she could not tell,—
except that every time she felt the slightest desire
to go into the forest, she saw the same hateful
faces which had peeped at her for the first time

when the cloud had passed over the face of the full
moon, and which had mocked at her from above
the soft mossy bed when it had been turned
into the stony wall which had forced them to go
forward, and she thought they forbade her to go
near them. But Aster, in spite of all her efforts
to detain him in the path, would sometimes run
away from her, saying he saw some beautiful
flower which he must gather, or else some sweet
child-face which smiled upon him; but each time
that he did this, he was sure to hasten back to
Eva, saying that either thorns had pierced or else
nettles stung him; and then he would hide his
face in the folds of Eva's white dress, trembling,
and saying that THEY were there, and had frightened him.

Still, Eva could never find out from the boy
who THEY were. For Aster, though he sometimes tried, could not tell her; it seemed as if he
was not allowed to speak, and the child began to
think that the faces which haunted her, and THEY
of whom Aster so often spoke, were only different
manifestations of the same power, which seemed
to follow them wherever they went, seeking an

E 4

opportunity to hurt them, although as yet no harm had been done.

Once, before Aster grew so small, Eva asked him why it was that they were thus followed.

"It is not you that THEY are following; THEY would do me harm if I were to fall into their hands; but I am safe while you keep me. You are beyond their reach."

But, though Aster knew this, it seemed to Eva that he dared, and tried, to put himself in the power of THEY, whom he seemed to dread,—for it was only when the faces looked at her from behind tree or shrub that Aster desired to leave her, and only then that he spoke of THEY who always frightened him back to her side. He never alluded to the flower they sought; only once, when Eva asked him what it was like, he said to her:

"I cannot describe it to you; you will know it when you see it."

"How shall I know it?" Eva asked.

"You will know it when the time comes."

But, though Eva looked carefully for the flower, she never saw it. There were flowers enough along the path, but the right one was not to be seen. She did not know—how could she?—that the search was only begun, and that not till after long wanderings and many troubles to Aster would she be able to find for him the flower which he had lost, and without which he could never regain his home.

CHAPTER VII.

ASTER'S MISFORTUNES.

T last, even the thin crescent of the moon disappeared, and once more Aster lay motionless, and, as it were, without life, the same tiny, helpless thing which Eva had taken from the crest of the fountain. Once more she wandered, alone,—for what companionship could she find in the senseless little figure which she carried about with her?—through the strange, dream-like country in which she now found herself. But, wherever she went, a feeling she could not explain nor understand made her hold the helpless little prince close, never for a moment letting him pass from her loving clasp.

Once more, too, the faint earth-light shone, instead of the vanished moon. And Eva thought that while Aster lay helpless, there were fewer

"As day by day the path led them on into the forest, the trees altered their shape."

Page 53.

difficulties in her path; the faces no longer
appeared to torment and harass her; the way
seemed easier to her feet; more and brighter
flowers bloomed along the path; and the misty,
shadowy shapes which were to be seen at intervals passing among the close-set trunks of the
trees were fair and lovely to look upon.

But this quiet was not to last. Again, after a
time, the music rang triumphantly through the
forest; and again, as the young moon sprang to
her station overhead, Aster awoke, to all appearance unconscious of the time he had slept, and of
the distance which Eva had carried him. As he
grew, with the moon, it seemed to her that he
was changed; that he was no longer the gentle,
loving boy who had wandered with her when the
first moon shone : something elfish, imp-like, and
changeable had come over him.

Then, too, as day by day the path led them on
into the forest, which seemed endless, the trees
altered their shape. Sometimes they were circled
with huge, twining snakes, which Eva thought
seemed coiled there, ready to seize her as she
passed, though when near them they proved to be

nothing but huge vines climbing up the trees. Here and there in the path lay huge stones, which you might think at first sight were insurmountable, obstructing their further progress; yet, if either Eva's foot touched them, or the hem of her white dress brushed ever so lightly against them, they would always fade away, like a shadow, into utter nothingness, or else would roll slowly away to one side, leaving the path clear. But when Aster saw the stones he would cry, and say that they would crush him if he passed them, and the only way in which Eva could soothe him was by taking him up in her arms and carrying him past the stones, while he hid his face, so as not to see them, in her long, golden curls.

Every now and then, in spite of what he had often told Eva,—that she, and she only, could find and give him the flower which he had lost,— Aster would declare to her that he saw it blooming in places where she saw nothing but nettles or ugly weeds, but which he would always insist were beds of the most beautiful flowers. These flowers, he said, called to him to come and gather them; while Eva thought that warning voices bade her pass them by, and that she saw over or else among them shadows of the same hateful faces which she dreaded. But it was useless to try and convince Aster of this; she soon learned that nothing ever presented the same appearance to him that it did to her.

In consequence, whenever Aster insisted upon leaving the path, as he often did, Eva watched him with a kind of terror, and never felt he was safe unless she led him by the hand. Placed, as he was, under her care, she felt sure that when with her no danger could come near him, nothing harm him. Still, if he had enemies in this great forest, he had friends, too; for once, when he stooped to gather a flower which bloomed near the path, she heard it say:

> "Guard thou well thy charge to-day,
> There is danger in the way."

But Aster laughed joyfully, as he looked up without gathering the flower, and said:

"Did you hear what the flower told me, Eva? That was the reason why I did not pick it, for it said that I should have much pleasure to-day."

Eva only smiled; she said nothing; she had
learned that Aster would not bear being contra-
dicted. But she quietly resolved to be more
watchful than ever; for, from what she had heard
the flower say, she thought that efforts would be
made to take the little prince from her.

She was wrong, however, for the day passed,
the moon disappeared, and, as nothing had happened to disturb them, she began to think that
perhaps she had been mistaken, and that Aster
had been right regarding the words which the
flower had spoken; for he had, all that day, been
cheerful and gentle. But, that night, she was
awakened from her sleep by Aster's talking, as
though to himself, in a rambling, disconnected
manner, of THEY whom he seemed to fear; and
this being the first time for days—not since he
had awakened from the stupor into which the disappearance of the moon had thrown him—that he
had mentioned or even appeared to think of these
nameless yet formidable beings, she guessed,
seeing that Aster's words were spoken, as it were,
in a dream, and unconsciously to himself, that
the coming day contained more danger to him
than any of the preceding ones.

It was, notwithstanding, with a feeling of relief
that Eva at last saw the moon arise, and once
more she and Aster set out on their journey. He
never referred to the words which had awakened
her. No strange sights or sounds came to disturb
them. There was utter stillness all around; and
as hour after hour passed, and Aster walked quietly
by her side, Eva began to think that her anxiety
had all been for nothing, and she relaxed a little
of her watchfulness.

At last they came to a place where every plant
along the path was hung with filmy, gossamer,
delicate webs, and in each web sat a spider. And
every spider was different,—no two of them being
alike. And, as they passed these patient spinners,
Aster clung closely to Eva's hand, saying that he
was afraid of being entangled among their webs,
or else stung by them; although to her it appeared
as though the spiders did not even notice them as
they passed. Then all of a sudden the webs and
the insects were gone; and the children saw crawling slowly in the path, as if it was afraid of them
and wanted to get out of their way, a spider larger
than any of those they had seen; a spider whose

body was ringed with scarlet and gold, whose long, slender black legs shone like polished jet, and whose eyes were like bright-green emeralds; a spider handsome enough to be the king of all the spiders.

And while Eva was admiring the beautiful colors of the insect, Aster let go her hand, and, stooping down, passed his finger gently over its gold and scarlet back.   Then the spider raised its head, and looked at Eva with its bright-green eyes, which, as Eva gazed at them, appeared to grow larger and brighter, and dazzled her own; and then a mist seemed to come over them, and everything began to fade slowly away; and she never noticed how Aster went, slowly, nearer and nearer to the insect, crouching down into the path as he did so, nor how the spider, by degrees, began to grow larger, and moved towards the side of the path, till a sudden cry from Aster, "Eva! Eva! help me!" roused her from the trance in which she stood, in which she saw nothing but the emerald eyes, like two gleaming lights; and then she saw that the beautiful spider had enveloped Aster in a large web which it had spun around him, and was

dragging him off the path, to carry him away
with it.

But Eva was not going to lose her charge.
Springing forward, she threw her arms around
him. And as her dress touched the web, it fell
off, releasing him; and the spider, unfolding a
pair of blue wings, flew into the forest with a loud
cry of disappointment; and as it flew away, its
shape changed, and Eva, looking after it, with her
arms still around Aster, saw that it had one of the
terrible faces which she had seen so often before.
Then it disappeared, and the two went on, or
rather tried to go on, for Aster complained that
his feet were fastened to the ground; and then
Eva saw that they were still tangled in some of the
spider's web; and both Eva and Aster tried in
vain to break it. But Eva was nearly in despair,
when, as she stooped, one of her long golden
curls brushed against the web, and then it melted
away and vanished like smoke.

Then, and not till then, were they able to go
on. But Aster walked forward unwillingly, and
complained that he was tired, and began to insist
upon Eva's stopping to rest. But she felt that

they would not be safe until after the moon was gone, and so they went on. At every mossy stone, every fair cluster of flowers, Aster would insist upon stopping, but Eva would not listen to him, for she always heard, at these places, a friendly voice which said, "Go on, go on;" and so they went on.

But at last Aster, who did nothing but complain of weariness, told Eva that he could and would go no farther. Seeing a great, velvety, green mushroom growing in the path, he ran and sat down upon it, saying that it was a seat which had been made and put there for him, and that Eva should not share it.

He had scarcely said this, had scarcely seated himself, when the mushroom changed into a great green frog, which, with Aster seated astride upon its back, began to hop nimbly away in the direction of the forest. But Eva, whose eyes had never for a moment left the boy, sprang forward, and before Aster—pleased at the motion of the frog—could say a word, she had dragged him off his strange steed, which turned and snapped at her, but, instead of touching her, caught the skirt of

Aster's coat in his mouth'and held on to it till Eva's efforts tore it from him, leaving, however, a small piece of the velvet in the frog's mouth. Even then he tried to seize Aster again, and it was not till Eva's dress touched him that he turned to leave them, still holding in his mouth the scrap torn from Aster's coat, and as he hopped off the path he faded away just like a shadow.

Then, too, the moon sank from the sky, and the two children, completely worn out, lay down and slept, and Eva knew that for a little while, at least, Aster was safe, because as she lay down she heard a little song which said:

> Tranquil be your sleep,
>   Peaceful be your rest,
> We a watch will keep,
>   Naught shall you molest;
>   Sleep, Eva, sleep.
>
> Where our light may shine,
>   Where we weave our charm,
> In our magic line,
>   Naught may cause you harm;
>   Sleep, Aster, sleep.

Then all was still. But though Eva, trusting to this song, was not afraid to lie down and sleep,

F

she never knew that while they did sleep a circle
of tiny shining lamps, like fairy-lamps, gleamed
all around them,—a magic circle which nothing
could pass. And although both the spider and
the green frog returned, bringing with them the
piece of Aster's coat, by means of which they
hoped to steal him away from Eva while he was
asleep, they could not pass the circle which the
Light Elves had drawn around the sleeping pair,
and, after many vain efforts to cross it, they vanished.

And the grateful elves had watched and saved
Aster because Eva, that morning, seeing a shape-
less, helpless worm lying near a stone, which was
about to fall and crush it, had tenderly picked up
the worm, and laid it carefully on a cool, green
leaf, out of danger. The grateful Light Elf,—for
such she was,—being compelled to wear the form
of a worm while the moonlight lasted, had come
with her companions to return what service she
could and give Eva a peaceful rest.

So, as ever, Good overcomes Evil, and no service, no matter how small or how trifling it may
seem, is ever wasted or thrown away.

CHAPTER VIII.

WHAT ASTER DID.

THE farther the progress which the children made into the forest, the wilder and more singular became the country through which they passed. Shadows cast by no visible forms went before them in the path,—shadows which shook, moved, and trembled ; which seemed as if they might all at once become real forms; shadows which had something dreadful about them, so that Eva was glad they were always in advance of her, and that her foot never had to touch the ground on which they lay. The color of the moon's light was changed. She shone with a pale greenish lustre. No green plants, no beautiful flowers, grew in the stony, rocky soil through which their path now lay. It produced things like sticks full of thorns. Under the stones lay hidden long, slender lizards,

(63)

or coiled-up serpents with forked and fiery-red tongues; things like dry twigs, which would suddenly display many legs and run away. Slow-crawling, hairy caterpillars, and round, fat, slimy worms, lay everywhere. Things like insects, which yet had no life, grew, instead of flowers, on the thorny sticks which stood among the stones. One of these things, in shape like a drag-on-fly, Aster picked; but he immediately dropped it, and said that it had stung him; and from that time Eva thought that he became more and more perverse, and that he was every day less like the gentle, affectionate boy she had been so glad to receive as a companion. She saw, too, that, while her own dress retained its spotless whiteness which nothing seemed to affect, his became every day more and more soiled and stained.

She missed, too, the low, sweet songs which had been sung by the flowers. To be sure, she had not always been able to distinguish their words, but they had been friendly, and had warned her of every danger before it came; but this was all over. Every night, as soon as the moon was gone, creatures like bats, with shining heads, came in

great numbers, flying around, and moaning in a
sad, mournful way which was most pitiful to hear.

As the moon neared the full, stranger shadows
and shapes came near. Yet the two went on, following the path, though Eva sometimes imagined
that the inhabitants of this strange country were
opposed to their passing through it. The music
which had been always heard at the rising and setting of the moon grew fainter and fainter, till at
last her ascent and fall came in perfect silence.
Then the strange shadows disappeared, but the
path led through a stonier and more rocky country, where all was wild and barren, and where,
after the moon was gone, little, dancing flames
played on the stones. Sometimes it was hard, indeed almost impossible, for the two children to
climb over the rough places in their path; and
Aster was very often discouraged; but Eva persevered, for she felt that the flower they sought could
never be found in this barren and dreary land.

I have said that Aster became every day more
obstinate and perverse. Sometimes Eva thought
that the strange flower, like a dragon-fly, which
he had picked, and which he said stung him, had

changed him, and that was the reason why he tried to annoy her in every possible way. He knew how uneasy she was when he was not with her; yet, knowing this, it was his greatest delight to hide himself behind some large stone, and after she had looked for him for a long time without finding him, afraid that his enemies had carried him off, he would jump out upon her with a loud mocking cry; he would pull her hair, he would try to soil her white dress, by throwing mud and dirt upon it, to make it, as he said, like his own, which was all stained and soiled, and then, when he found that he could not discolor its whiteness, he would throw himself down on the ground, and kick and scream, and tell Eva that he hated her, and that he wished THEY would come and carry her away.

One day, when Aster had been worse than ever, and the way had been stonier and harder than it had ever been before, Eva began to think that it was of no use to go on, or to look for the flower lost so long ago by the imp-like boy, whose powers of annoying her seemed to increase as he grew smaller with the moon. She sat down upon one of the rough stones, and great tears gathered in her eyes. And as, one by one, they rolled down her cheeks and fell to the ground, everything around her seemed to grow vague and dim; and at her feet, just where the tear-drops fell, there came a bed of round green leaves, under whose shelter bloomed and nodded a multitude of tiny purple flowers; violets, whose sweet fragrance, rising, made a misty cloud, through which Eva caught faint glimpses of a pond, and a house near it, and then the house seemed to change into a cosy parlor. And by the window of this parlor a lady was sitting sewing, and rocking a cradle with her foot, and singing to a baby boy who was kicking and crowing in the cradle; and then the child heard her mother's voice calling, softly, "Eva, Eva!" But before these memories came fully back, Aster came up, and angrily crushed and trampled the sweet violets under his feet; and as he did so the cloud and its pictures disappeared, and Eva forgot them; only she was very sorry for the dear little flowers that Aster had killed.

Poor little flowers, which tried to do her good!

For it seemed to her that with their last breath
of perfume there came a low voice, which whispered. "Beware of the stones,"—and that was
all. And then she asked Aster why he had de-
stroyed the harmless flowers, which had only come
to warn them.

"They only came to do me harm," Aster said,
angrily. "They would have taken you away from
me, and I should never have seen you again. You
shall not go away from me yet, for I can never
get home without you; after I have done with
you, why, then you may go."

"Where?" Eva asked, pained at this selfish
speech.

"Into what is to be,—out of Shadow-Land into
what is to come, but is not yet."

"I do not understand you."

"You will know when the time comes. I
crushed the flowers because they were part of
what is to come; they had no right here."

Nothing more was said; but Aster seemed rest-
less and uneasy until they left the place where
the violets had bloomed. Yet nothing disturbed
them, and on they went, till Eva began to wonder

where the stones could be of which the voice had said, '' Beware !''

At last, when there was only a tiny crescent of the moon, like a faint silver line, floating in the sky, and Aster's figure, like it, was once more reduced to its smallest dimensions, the forest through which they had wandered for so long ended; and as they passed from it, a low cry of surprise from Aster made Eva look down, as she saw that his eyes were fixed upon the earth; and then she saw with equal surprise that, while she walked along the rough, stony path without leaving any impression, every step that Aster took left a deep, plain track, and that in each of these tracks there was either a frog or a spider, which would disappear while she looked at them.

Then a sudden turn in the path brought them to a place where a huge pile of rocks, like an immense stone wall built by giants, rose up before them. A faint breath of violets seemed to come, and then pass away, and as it did, Eva knew that these were the stones of which she had been warned.

At that very moment there was a flash of

light, and a star fell from the sky, near the moon.

"A falling star, how pretty it is!" Eva said, as she watched the bright thing, which seemed to fall behind the stone wall. " Did you see it, Aster?"

"You don't know anything, Eva," was his reply. "I told you once before that everything which was lost in the moon fell into Shadow-Land, and that was something bright which fell just now."

But this had nothing to do with the wall, which must be climbed. How, Eva did not know. She was almost afraid to try it; and so she stood, looking at it, when Aster, who, ever since he had crushed the violets, had followed her in silence, except when he had spoken of the shooting star, with his eyes bent on the ground, suddenly ran forward to the wall, and began to look eagerly into every crevice between the stones.

"What are you looking for?" Eva asked him. "Come back to me, Aster; it is not safe for you there without me."

"I will look," Aster said. "The bright thing

you called a star was my flower. It is here, and I am going to find it."

"Don't!" Eva said, imploringly, as the boy tried to creep into one of the crevices between the stones. "Remember, Aster, that the moon is nearly gone, and if she should disappear, you will go to sleep, and then you will have to stay in there until she returns."

"I don't care!" Aster said, crossly. "If, as I know I shall, I find my flower in here, the moon will have no more power over me, for I shall then be myself; and you may go on alone into what will come. Besides, the piece which was torn off my coat is in there, and I am going to get it. If I do go to sleep, I can lie down in here, and rest; you can mark the place and wait for me, if you choose. I don't intend to obey you any longer; you are nothing but a little girl, and I am a prince."

Eva's hand was on Aster's shoulder, and when he found she would not remove it, he raised his own, and struck her. Not till then did the child unwillingly release him, seeing that all her efforts to detain him would be in vain. Then, without saying another word, Aster crept slowly into the crevice. And Eva, picking up a white stone which lay at her feet, made a mark over the place with it. As she did this, the faint silver light of the moon faded from the sky; there was a loud croaking as of frogs, and then she heard the shrill cry of the spider which had spun the web around Aster; and then it grew very dark, and a sudden drowsiness came over her, which she could not resist; and, lying down upon a stone under the crevice into which Aster had crept, Eva fell asleep.

CHAPTER IX.

THE DOOR IN THE WALL.

IT was with a start that, after the darkness had gone, Eva awoke from the dull, heavy sleep into which she had fallen; and for a moment she could not recollect how it was that she should be lying upon a stone at the foot of this huge rocky wall, or why she should be alone, without Aster near her. She looked for him, thinking that perhaps he might have hidden himself, only to tease her; but he was nowhere to be found. She called him, hoping that he might hear and answer her; but there was no reply,—only the rocks echoed back the sound of her own voice, which said, "Aster, Aster! where are you?" and then another echo seemed to answer, mockingly, "Where?"

G

But all this only lasted for a few moments. Then all at once Eva remembered the falling star; the warning which the violets had given her; the blow, which, coming as it did from Aster's hand, had so deeply grieved her; her efforts to detain him at her side, which had all proved useless; and how, after the boy had crept into one of the crevices of the wall, declaring he went there in search of his flower, she had picked up a stone, which she now found she still held in her hand, and marked the place. Then she felt relieved, for she knew that this was the time when Aster would be asleep, as he always was when the moon was absent, and consequently he could not move from the place into which he had crept. She thought, therefore, that, whenever she chose, she would find him, and, taking him again under her care, carry him away from this barren and stony waste.

Encouraged and relieved by this thought, she did not look for Aster any longer, but went to a little spring bubbling up between two rough stones, and which was the only pleasant thing she could see in this rocky place. She knelt down by it, for she was thirsty, to drink from its cool and sparkling waters, and then to wash her face and hands in them ; and as she dipped her hands in the spring, the little ripples they made whispered, softly, " Over yonder ! over yonder !" but Eva was not sure if she really had heard these words, or only imagined them. .

Refreshed by the cool water, she went back to the great, rough, stone wall, intending to secure her charge, and then try to go on. But what was her surprise, on returning, as she thought, to the same stone on which she had slept, to see that there were so many stones just exactly like it, that she could not find the one she wanted ! and, what was still stranger, she saw that over every little hole, every tiny cavity in the stone, there was a white mark exactly like the one which she had made over the crevice into which Aster had crept, and she could not say which of them all was hers.

She was in despair for a moment. How was she to find, among all these holes, each with the same white mark over it, the one in which Aster was asleep? Then she remembered that standing still and looking at the wall would do no good ;

that if she wanted to find Aster she must look for him; and Eva determined to examine every hole she saw, in hopes that with patience and perseverance she might at last succeed in finding her lost charge, of whom, in spite of all the trouble he had given her, she had grown very fond.

But if she had been surprised at seeing a white mark over every hole, instead of the one she had made, she was still more astonished when she saw that in every cranny which she examined there sat either a large·black-legged spider, with a gold and scarlet back, and eyes which shone in the dark like little bright stars, or else there squatted snugly in it a huge green frog, with a wide mouth and projecting black eyes; while just beyond her reach there would flutter every now and then a little green flag, like the scrap of velvet, as Eva thought, which the teeth of the frog had torn from Aster's coat.

Yet the child climbed slowly up the wall, fearless of the spiders and the frogs, which she knew had no power to harm her, even if they had wished it. But seeing them, and knowing, as she did, that these two creatures, in the forest through

which they had passed, had tried to get possession
of Aster, Eva began to fear that by creeping into
the hole he had put himself in their power, and
that she would never be able to find him again.

She went on, however, looking carefully into
every tiny cavity, but always with the same result.
No Aster was to be seen: only huge spiders and
squatting frogs stared at her from every cranny.
And, as she climbed up higher and higher, she
found that the rocky wall was like a giant stair-
case; and when she looked back, noticing that
the stones she displaced, as she climbed up, only
rolled a short time and then made no noise as
they fell, and thinking that after her search was
over she would return to the little spring and
wait there patiently until the moon rose again,
when, as she hoped, Aster, if she did not find him
now, would wake up and come back to her, she
saw that she could never return to the spring.
For the steps by which she had come were gone,
melting one by one into the face of the rock,
changing into a steep precipice behind her; and
at its foot were curling mists and vapors, among
which she saw dimly the hateful, mocking faces

she had seen before. Go back she could not, for every step, as she passed it, melted into the precipice ; to look back made her dizzy. She must go upward.

For the first time since she had begun to climb the wall, which had changed, as she climbed, into steps, and then into a precipice, Eva was afraid. But there was no choice left for her ; go on she must ; and, accordingly, on she went, till she came to a place where the rock rose, so high that she could not see its top, in a smooth, unbroken wall, over which she could not possibly climb, and a narrow path ran along its base ; and as yet she had not seen nor heard anything of the truant Aster.

She walked slowly along the foot of the great blank wall, tired and discouraged. What to do now, she did not know. She could not go back, for there was the frightful precipice ; in front was the wall, along which she was walking. Poor Eva was almost ready to cry, when all of a sudden she saw a door, cut in the stone, and the door was shut. But she heard, behind this door, the silvery voices and ringing laughter of children, and then a great longing came over her to go in and join them, and she thought that perhaps Aster might be with them.

Yet, although she tried, she could not open the door. She heard the merry voices of the children, and, hearing them as plainly as she did, she thought it was strange that they did not hear her and open the door to her; for, try as she would, she could not open it. And then she grew tired of trying, and would have gone on, when, looking once more at the door to see if there was any way of opening it which she could possibly have neglected, she saw cut across the door, in deep, old-fashioned, moss-grown letters, the word

Knock.

Then, gathering courage, Eva raised her tiny hand, and knocked. Once, and no answer came. Again, and with the same result. A third time, and then the merry voices of the children, and their gay laughter, ceased, and Eva hoped that her appeal was heard.

CHAPTER X.

THE VALLEY OF REST.

EVA waited for a moment, with as much patience as she could, in hopes that the door might now be opened for her. Vain hopes, for the ringing laughter and the merry voices began again ; and once more Eva would have been discouraged, if the thought had not come that perhaps her gentle knocking had not been heard, and once more she tapped, louder this time, at the door.

A voice within immediately asked, " Who knocks?"

' I—Eva," was the child's reply.

" Eva may enter."

Poor child ! She thought the permission was useless, for the door remained as tightly shut as ever.

"Why do you not come in?" the same voice asked, after a pause. "You are permitted."

"I cannot come in, because the door is shut," Eva said.

"Take the key and unlock it."

But Eva, after looking around carefully, could see no key, and so she said, "I do not know where the key can be."

"Look under your right foot," said the voice within; and Eva, stepping to one side, saw lying, just where her foot had been, a queer little key, which she picked up; and seeing a key-hole among the quaint letters of the inscription, she found the little key just fitted it; and on turning it, the door flew open, and, as it did, a band of beautiful children came forward to meet her, though not one of them crossed the threshold of the door, and they bade her welcome. But when Eva would have gone in, it seemed to her that invisible hands prevented her entrance; and then one of the children, seeing that she still held in her hand the white stone she had picked up near the spring, and with which she had made the mark over Aster's hiding-place, told her to throw it away, for that

6

nothing from Shadow-Land could be brought into their valley; and then to be careful and not touch the threshold of the door, but to step over it. And Eva did as they told her; but when she threw the white stone over the precipice, it changed into a large white moth as it left her hand; and Eva, watching it, saw one of the faces rise from out of the curling mists to meet it, and then the moth changed into a face like the one she had first seen,-and then both disappeared among the mists and vapors. And the moment she passed through the door, it closed suddenly behind her, and could not be told from the solid rock; and Eva saw that she was in a place totally different from anything she had ever seen before in her wanderings.

She found that she was now in a large, grassy valley, in the midst of which was built a beautiful rose-colored palace, shining like a star. Flowers of the gayest hues bloomed all through the grass; fountains of musical water, surrounded with rainbows, played here and there; birds and butterflies of brilliant colors flew among the flowers, and were so tame that they would alight on the children's hands, and the birds were so wise that they could talk, and tell the most interesting stories, which you never grew tired of hearing. A little brook ran sparkling through the valley, and groups of beautiful children were playing on its banks, among whom Eva looked—but looked in vain— for Aster.

The children gathered around her, asking where she came from, if she was the Queen who was to reign over them, and if she was not going to live always with them. And when Eva tried to explain how she had come, and asked them if they knew where Aster was, they joined hands and danced in a circle around her to their own singing, and then one of them gave her the leaves of a flower to eat. Now the leaves of this flower were delicious, and as sweet as honey to the taste, and one never wearied of eating them; and as Eva ate them, all memory of Shadow-Land and of Aster faded from her mind, and she was content to remain in the valley with the children.

It was a pleasant life that she led in this peaceful valley, surrounded, as it was, and shut in by high, insurmountable, and steep rocks, over which

nothing without wings could go; in which the
children dwelt, and where there was neither sun
nor moon, but only a soft, rosy light, which never
hurt or dazzled the eyes, and where nothing ever
happened which could disturb the peace of the
place.   To chase the brilliant butterflies, to listen
to the songs and stories of the birds, to dance on
the soft green grass, and gather flowers to make
fragrant wreaths and garlands with which to deco-
rate the beautiful palace in which, when darkness
came over the valley, they all assembled, and
where tables, spread with the most delicious fruits,
always stood ready for them,—such was the life
that Eva and the children led in the Valley of
Rest.

But at last a day came when the children told
Eva that, as their custom was, they must leave the
valley and carry baskets of flowers and fruit to the
Queen for whom they had at first taken her. She
could not go with them now, they said, but the
next time that they went they would take her with
them. They would be gone the next morning
before she was awake, and she would be alone for
that day in the valley; but then they would return;

and the only favor they asked of her was this,—
that she would not go near the brook, nor play
upon its banks, while they were absent.

Eva willingly promised this. Such a little thing
as it was to promise, when she would have the
whole fair valley to herself, to go where she pleased,
and to do what she pleased! It would be very
easy to keep away from the brook.

But when once more the soft, rosy light came,
and the darkness was gone, and Eva awoke to
find herself lying, all alone, on her little bed in
the palace, and to know that all the children were
indeed gone, though only for a time, a strange
restlessness came over her, and she felt that she
could not stay all alone in the palace. She would
go out of it into the valley. But she was no better
off there. She gathered flowers and made beautiful wreaths and bouquets, but there was no one to
admire them when they were made. The rainbows around the fountains were less brilliant; the
birds were all gone with the children, so that she
could not listen to their songs or the stories they
might have told her. She might play and dance,
but what fun was there in that, when she had no

H

companions to dance and play with her? Eva
thought she never had spent such a stupid, long,
dull day in all her life; and she wished it was
over. The only thing which seemed as merry as
ever was the little brook, which she had promised
to avoid, yet which rippled along so joyously that
it was as much as Eva could do to keep away
from it.

But she remembered her promise to the children,
and turning her back upon the brook, she went
and sat down near one of the fountains. She had
only been there for a few moments, when she felt
something pull her dress; and looking round to
see what it was,—wondering if the children could
possibly have returned,—she saw, to her great surprise, a huge green toad, which had hold of her
dress, and which, when she looked at it, said:

"Croak! croak!"

Then Eva knew that she had seen the toad
before, and she began to wonder how it had
gotten into the Valley of Rest, where she never
had seen anything like it. But she did not have
much time for wonder; for the toad, giving her
dress another pull, said to her, "Come to the

brook! Come to the brook!" And then it began to hop towards the brook just as fast as it could go.

She forgot her promise to the children, and, just exactly as she had done once before, she obeyed the toad, and went down to the brook. And when she got there, she could not imagine why the toad wanted her to go there, for he was nowhere to be seen, and the brook looked just as it always did. But she sat down by it, and watched the merry water as it rippled along over its pebbly bed. Then, soothed by the low murmur it made, she lay down on the grass and fell asleep. And while she was asleep she had a dream; and this is what she dreamed:

She saw Aster, his dress torn, dirty, and ragged, his long curls tangled; tired and sad, and compelled to carry burdens of stone too heavy for him to lift. And when he wanted to rest, two figures, with the faces which Eva had seen in the forest and among the curling mists and vapors at the foot of the precipice, beat him with rods full of thorns. And then a huge red-and-black spider would sting him in the foot, or a great green frog, with prominent black eyes, would threaten to swallow him; and then the boy would cry, and call for Eva to come and help him.

Then the frog would say:

"Why did you let me tear your coat?"

And the faces would ask:

"Why did you lose your flower?"

And then the spider would say:

"Why did you creep into the rock?"

And to all this Aster would only answer with the cry, "Eva! Eva! help me!"

Then one of the faces said, angrily:

"We shall punish you here until three things are done, because through three things you fell into our power. First. Eva must find your coat. Second. She must get the piece to mend it with. Third. She must find you. But you need not call her, because she cannot hear you; for she is in the Valley of Rest with the Happy Children, who are the Dawn Fairies, and she has forgotten you. And there are many dangers to pass in Shadow-Land before she can come to you; and she will not come, unless she hears you call."

Then they would beat him again; and Aster

would cry, louder than ever, "Eva! Eva! help me!"

And then the dream passed away, and Eva awoke. And it seemed to her that Aster's voice mingled with the rippling of the water, and it cried, piteously, "Eva! Eva! help me!"

And then Eva knew why it was that the children had begged her not to go near the brook while they were gone; because its voice would bring back to her all that she had forgotten. For now, as she sat by it, she remembered everything that the leaves of the flower which she had eaten had made her forget; and she sprang to her feet, determined to follow the course of the brook, and let it lead her to where Aster was.

She went all through the fair valley, along the margin of the brook with whose waters Aster's voice still seemed to mingle. It led her at last to the high rocks, which, like a steep wall, surrounded the valley, and where a low cavern, the roof of which was only a few inches above the surface of the water, received the brook. Eva could not enter it, neither could she climb the steep precipice-like wall; and, with Aster's voice still sound-

ing piteously in her ears, with a heavy heart, after
several fruitless efforts to climb the rocks, she
went back to the palace, determined to wait for
the return of the children; for, although she had
been very happy while with them, and was un-
willing to leave them, she intended to ask them
how she could leave the peaceful Valley of Rest,
and if they would provide her with the means of
continuing her search for Aster.

Had Eva consulted her own wishes, and been
able to carry them out, she would not have waited
one moment, but would have gone at once out
into Shadow-Land, which she now knew lay all
around the valley. She knew, too, that the little
brook running through the valley, and which had
brought her Aster's cry for help, was the same
whose "Follow, follow me!" had led her to the
golden fountain from whose crest she had received her little charge. But how to leave the
valley she did not know. She could do nothing
by herself,—she must wait till the return of the
children,—so that she could scarcely be patient till
the hours of darkness came, knowing that during

them, and before the soft, rosy light could dawn again, that they would be with her.

There was nothing for it, however, but patience, and at last, after a day which had seemed at least a year long, darkness covered the valley; and although Eva had fully intended to keep awake until the children's return, her eyes, try and resolve as she might, would not stay open, and she slept.

CHAPTER XI.

THE MAGIC BOAT.

MORNING came, and Eva awoke, to find that she was all alone in the palace, and to wonder at the utter stillness around her. There was no song of birds to be heard,— no fall of musical waters,—no merry children's ringing laughter and sweet voices. To all intents and purposes the palace seemed as deserted as it had been the day before. And wondering at all this, Eva rose, and went out of the palace to look for her companions.

They had returned; but when she saw them she understood why everything was so still. For, instead of the merry songs and joyous games and dances with which they had been accustomed to begin the day, they were gathered in little groups, and every face wore a sad and mournful expres-

sion. They seemed troubled, and every now and
then one of them would point to the brook, and
then shake her head; and Eva was going to ask
them what could possibly have happened, and
what the matter was, when they saw her; and
then the whole crowd came around her, and before she could say a word, they exclaimed, with
one voice:

"Oh, Eva! Eva! what have you done? You
forgot your promise; you went to the brook, and
you heard its story?"

Then it came into Eva's mind that she must
leave the children, who seemed so sorry for what
she had done, and she hung her head and said,
timidly:

"I could not help it."

"It is true, and only what we feared," one of
them said,—the same one who had spoken to Eva
through the door. "We knew how it would be
before we left you. You could not help it, for it
was Fate, and no promise can bar the power, no
wishes change the will, of Fate."

Then Eva began to tell them her story. And
they all listened, and when she told them how the

green toad had pulled her dress, another of the children spoke and told Eva that the green toad was Aster's friend, and would do all it could to help him. That, just before she came to the valley, it had been there and told them she was coming. And then Eva finished her story, and begged them to let her go.

"We cannot keep you," they said to her, "even if we wished it. We would like to keep you with us, but the green toad has commanded us to help you, so far as lies in our power. But we cannot save you from the dangers of the way. THEY, who are more powerful than our Queen, have forbidden it, and will not allow us to tell you what these dangers are, or how you can avoid them or escape them. That you will learn on the Enchanted River, down which you will have to go, and we must, if you ask us, furnish you with the means of reaching it. You cannot go there unless we help you, and we cannot keep you here if we would."

"Will I find Aster?" Eva asked.

"That will depend upon yourself," one of the children said, exactly as if she was telling a story she had heard. "If Aster had obeyed you, as he should have done, and as he was expected to do, your journey would have ended here, in this Valley of Rest, and we, who are the Dawn Fairies, would have been able to take his flower from the Night and Shadow Elves; but the loss of part of his coat gave them power over him, because Darkness always swallows up Light whenever it can; and so, just at the entrance of this place, on the verge between Shadow and Dawn, they succeeded in luring him away from you."

Then they told Eva that for a certain time, which had now expired, Aster's enemies had been able to prevent her seeking for him. "During that time," they went on, "we were permitted to receive you; but then since Aster's friends have been able to speak to you by means of the brook, though they can do nothing to rescue or to help him, for you are the only person who can release him from the power of the Elves of Shadow-Land; and since you have heard the voice, and are willing to follow it, we can only, much as we would like to keep you with us, help you, and let you go."

" Has she no choice?" another asked. "Could she not, if she chose, remain with us, instead of exposing herself to the dangers through which she must pass?"

"I would rather go," Eva began, "if I may choose."

"You are right," the first one who had spoken went on. "It is your fate, and," using, as Eva remembered, words that Aster had spoken long before, and which seemed to be a proverb among the elves and fairies, "it will be, because it must be."

And then Eva heard, above the voices of the children and mingling with them, the words which had come to her along the waters of the brook, but spoken this time more plaintively than ever:

"Eva! Eva! help me!"

And the children heard, for they said:

"You will not hear those words after you leave our valley. For, in the region through which you must pass, Aster's friends have no power; you will have to depend wholly upon yourself. And"—as the waters of the little brook, by whose margin they were standing, began to ripple along faster, and murmur louder, while the musical fountains began to play, and the birds to sing— "and now you must leave us: everything is in readiness, and the time has come."

Then, with Eva in their midst, the children began to walk slowly along the brook, which no longer brought Aster's voice with it. On they went, through the calm valley; not, however, as Eva had expected, to the door in the rock through which she had entered, and which she had never been able to find again,—though she had looked for it the day before, but in the opposite direction,—towards the cavern in which the waters of the brook disappeared. She asked why she was not to be allowed to seek for Aster among the rocky, stony wastes in which he had disappeared.

"Because that is all over, and you cannot go back into the Past," was the reply. "Nothing, which has once happened there, or been seen there, remains in Shadow-Land."

They had come, by this time, to the cavern, and Eva saw that its roof was higher above the

I 7

brook than it had been the day before; and that, floating on the water which was here as smooth and still as glass, there were a great many pure white lilies, and that every now and then a speckled trout would jump from the water, and send a shower of crystal drops to sparkle on the green leaves around the white lilies.

"There lies your way," the children said, pointing to the cavern and the brook. "But we must give you the means of going down the brook to the place where it meets the Enchanted River. Beyond that we cannot help you. We can only send you, in our boat, down the brook."

At these words Eva looked up in great surprise, for no boat was to be seen, and she could not imagine where one was to come from. But then one of the children clapped her hands, and, as she did so, a lily-bud slowly rose from the water, and then opened, till it was larger and whiter than any of the other lilies. And then, while all looked on in silence, the pure white leaves of the lily fell into the water and melted away in it like snow; and then another waved her hands in the air, and immediately, on the stalk from which the lily-petals had fallen, there grew a pod. And when the pod had stopped growing, a third, stooping by the brook, dipped her hands into the water, and the lily-pod detached itself from its stem, and came floating to the bank.

Then the one who had clapped her hands took the pod out of the water and laid it on the bank. The second opened it and taking from out of it six round speckled seeds, laid them in the hands of the third. Then the third threw these six seeds, one by one, into the water, and as each seed touched the water it changed into a beautiful, large speckled trout; and one by one the six trout, gently moving their fins, ranged themselves in a line, their heads to the bank, and remained there, waiting.

Then the three children, lifting up the empty lily-pod, placed it gently upon the brook, and Eva saw that, as it lay on the smooth waters, it had become a little boat. And then the six trout, one by one, swam from the line which they had formed, and ranged themselves around it, one at the bow and one at the stern, and two on each side; and while she looked at the tiny boat it grew longer and broader, and at either end it rose in a graceful curve, finished at bow and stern with an open lily-cup; and then the calm surface of the water broke into a thousand little ripples, rocking the lilies to and fro, which bent as though they were saluting the little vessel, along whose sides the tiny waves flowed caressingly.

The children then told Eva that everything was ready, and that it was time for her to enter the boat which they had prepared for her, and which the six Fish Fairies would guide down the brook. But Eva hesitated, for the boat, she thought, was too small for her. One of the children, seeing that Eva hesitated, told her not to be afraid, for the boat was built in such a way, being a magic boat, that it would hold any one for whom it was made. So Eva did as she was told, and, stepping lightly into the boat, she found that it was just the right size for her; though she did not exactly know if it was she that had grown smaller or the boat which had grown larger.

As she sat down, the children told her to be careful and eat nothing except what the trout, who were to guide the boat, would bring her; and in return she was to take care of them, and let no one molest them, for the Fish Fairies are the weakest of all the fairies, though they can go where the others dare not even be seen. When the boat had taken her as far as it could, it would leave her, and return to the Valley of Rest.

Then, all joining hands, the children began to sing; and this is what they sung:

> Little boat,
> Gently float,
> With your sweet freight laden;
> Evil charm
> May not harm
> Eva, the earth-maiden.

> On her way,
> Night and day,
> Bear her onward ever;
> Till she land
> On the strand
> Of th' Enchanted River.

On this spot
Linger not !
'Tis the appointed hour !
Little boat,
Onward float,
Led by magic power.

As the last words were sung, the boat, apparently of its own accord, moved into the centre of the brook, its bow pointing to the cavern. Then it paused for a moment, till the six speckled trout could come and take their places around it. And then, with a smooth, gliding motion, it went towards the entrance of the cavern, which suddenly raised its arch so as to admit the magic boat.   When it was just under the arch, the boat stopped for a moment, and as Eva looked back, she saw that the children were already going back to the palace, singing as they went,—the bright, rosy light, and the rainbow-surrounded fountains, and the beautiful birds, seemed more charming than ever in contrast with the Dark Unknown into which she was going.

Then the boat shot forward again, and the arch of the cavern, which had been raised to allow the boat to enter, dropped behind her like a curtain, shutting out the Valley of Rest from Eva's sight.

The rest she had enjoyed there was over,—her wanderings had again begun.

CHAPTER XII.

DOWN THE BROOK.

T was not without a moment's fear that Eva saw the arch of the cavern close behind her, shutting her into silence; and surrounding her with a darkness which could not only be seen, but which was almost to be felt. At least so it seemed in contrast with the bright valley which she had left; but before many minutes had passed, or the boat had gone very far, her eyes became accustomed to the change, the intense blackness which surrounded her softened into a pale, dim gray; and then Eva saw that she was in a low arched place, like a long tunnel cut in the solid rock. Every now and then a drop of water would fall splashing into the brook from the roof, or else a little wave would break, rippling against the wall; but those were the only sounds to be heard.

Even the boat glided along noiselessly, with a smooth, uniform motion,—and the tiny waves, which occasionally ruffled the surface of the dark, still water, passed under her without Eva's noticing them. Leaning over the side, Eva could just see in the water the dim outlines of the trout, which swam along noiselessly in their respective places. Then all at once it grew lighter, and in the two cups of the lilies in which the curved prow and stern of the boat ended, she saw that a pale, blue flame was burning, and she knew then that from these blue flames came all the dim gray light which illumined the cavern. And presently, without thinking, she dipped her hand into the brook, and right away the water all around it was full of bright sparkles, and yet these little sparkles did not burn her; and then one of the six speckled trout came and rubbed his head softly against Eva's hand, and asked her what she wanted.

Eva stroked the trout's back, and said,—

"Nothing."

"Well, when you do want anything," the trout

said to her, "just dip your hand into the water, and one of us will come to you. Then you must ask for what you want, and if we can get it for you we will; and when you are hungry we will bring you something to eat."

Eva thanked the trout, and said she would be sure to ask when she wanted anything. And then she took her hand out of the water, and the trout went back to his place, and Eva lay down quietly in the bottom of the boat, for she was tired of sitting up, and looked at the roof of the cavern. It was all rough and uneven, high above the water in some places and near it in others, with bright stones set here and there in it, which shone and sparkled like diamonds or little stars whenever the boat passed under them, or the light from the flames burning in the lily-cups, which Eva called her lamps, fell upon them. But there was no sign of life in the cavern, except that every now and then things like bats, frightened by the light, would fly out of holes in the wall away back into the darkness.

The boat went on and on, though there seemed no current in the water over which it glided, till,

as Eva thought, they must have travelled for days.
Sometimes she would sleep, and the boat went on
just the same; when she was hungry, she would
dip her hand into the water, and the trout would
bring her a basket filled with the fruit which grew
in the Valley of Rest. But Eva began to be very
tired of the long journey through the cavern; and
she was wondering to herself how much farther
they would have to go, when all of a sudden the
little blue flames burning in the lily-cups flickered
for a moment, and then, seemingly gathering
themselves together, shot up to the roof of the
cavern and disappeared, leaving everything again
in total darkness; and Eva was just going to ask
the trout what this meant, when she saw, far away
in the distance before her, what looked to her
like a tiny, yet beautiful blue star shining.

This little star, which was yet far away, seemed
so fair and lovely that Eva said, without intending to speak, "O little boat, if only you would
sail faster, and go near the pretty star!" And,
just as if the boat had heard and understood the
words, it began to move faster,—or was it the star
which grew larger and larger, and came to meet

them? No! it surely was no star, for the blue spot became larger and still larger, and then the cavern grew lighter and lighter, till, when she was near enough, Eva saw that what she had taken for a star was the arched entrance into the rock, and the light it shed was the pure light of day pouring into the darkness of the cavern.

But it did not look so very inviting when the boat came nearer. Beyond the arch the air was full of curling mists and vapors, like those which Eva had seen at the foot of the precipice, and through these mists and vapors she caught dim glimpses of the same old hateful faces she had seen so often before. Just before the boat reached the arch, one of the six trout, putting his head above the water, said to her:

"Stop the boat."

" How can I ?" Eva asked, in surprise.

"Speak to her ; she will obey you."

And, to Eva's great astonishment, as soon as the words, spoken very doubtingly, "Little boat, wait," passed her lips, the little vessel stopped, and lay without moving on the water.

Then the same trout which had spoken to her

previously put his head again out of the water and said :

"Before we go on, among the mists and vapors which lie beyond the cavern, it is well to tell you to be prepared. You must be on your guard, for THEY who dwell on the margin of the Brook of Mists will do everything in their power to prevent your reaching the Enchanted River. You will have to be careful, not only for yourself but for us, and no matter what they whom we meet may ask you to do, you must refuse, however trifling it may seem. Beyond the cavern we have no power to warn you; you must judge for yourself."

More than this, the trout went on, they were not permitted to say to her. So Eva thanked them, and promised to remember what they had told her; and then she told the little boat to go on, and once more the little vessel glided forward with each trout in its own place.

They proceeded slowly; the curling mists and vapors always before them,—and, as Eva noticed, always behind them, although they were never close to the boat,—just as if she carried a free

K

space along with her, and that the mists were not allowed to come within a certain distance of her.

So, for a time, they went quietly down the brook. And Eva, seeing that nothing happened, began to wonder why the trout had told her to be careful; and she was looking over the side of the boat at her own face reflected in the clear water, in which not a fish was to be seen, except those with her, when suddenly the boat began to rock to and fro, as she never had done before; and when Eva turned round to ascertain the cause of this rocking, there, perched on the side of the boat, was a great black jackdaw.

But, oh! what a very queer-looking jackdaw he was, to be sure! Every here and there he had peacock feathers stuck in among his plumage, and it was easy to see that they were only put in for show. It was as much as Eva could do to keep from laughing when she looked at him.

"Caw! caw!" cried the jackdaw, with his head to one side, just as if he thought himself the finest bird in the world. "I am hungry, little girl, for I have flown a long way to-day, and I want to know if you won't give me something to eat."

"I would, with pleasure," Eva said, "if I had any corn with me, for that is what jackdaws eat."

The jackdaw tossed his head at this.

"Pooh! you are silly; can't you see I'm a peacock? Just look at my fine feathers, and tell me what you suppose I want with corn? If you really are willing to give me something to eat, why, I'll take one of those fine, fat fish swimming near the boat."

"That I cannot let you do," Eva said. "I know who you are, now: you are the bird who stole the peacock's feathers; I saw a picture of you in a little book I once read."

"Found out! Found out!" cawed the jackdaw; and, with that, off he flew; and he was in such a hurry to be gone that he dropped two of the long feathers which had been in his tail, and Eva picked them up and stuck them into the side of the boat.

Then one of the trout, after the jackdaw was gone, put his head up out of the water and said:

"It is a good thing for all of us that you said 'no' to the bird. For, if you had said he might take one of us, he would not have touched us, but would have pecked a hole in the boat, and she would have sunk to the bottom of the brook. We should have had to leave you, and then you never could have reached the Enchanted River."

"Where is the Enchanted River?" Eva asked the trout.

He answered, "It runs through Shadow-Land."

"And where are we?"

"We are on the Brook of Mists, which empties into the Enchanted River. You came out of Shadow-Land when you entered the Valley of Rest."

Then the boat went on quietly again. Only for a time, however, and presently Eva heard a voice, in a squeaky tone, calling to her:

"Stop, little girl, and take me in."

And there, apparently crawling along the surface of the water, was a queer little dwarf. He had a large head, with round, green eyes; a fat, round body; and he was dressed in a yellow coat with scarlet facings, and his legs were so long and thin that they bent under him as he walked. And when he came up to the boat and laid his

_" Stop, little girl, and take me in "

hand upon it, Eva saw that it was not a hand, but only a sharp black claw.

"Take me in!" he repeated.

Eva peeped at the trout over the side of the boat before she answered him, but they were taking no notice of the dwarf, and were swimming along as quietly as ever.

"Take me in!" he squeaked again.

"No," Eva said; "the boat is too small to hold us both."

"Then give me one of those peacock feathers to fan myself with."

"I must refuse you," Eva went on; "but perhaps the jackdaw, who was here not long since, might supply you, as he did me."

"You are very unkind," the dwarf said. "Come, now, I will give you such a pretty flower if you will only let me go a little way with you; a star-flower. Aster means—a star."

Eva shook her head. "I cannot."

"Why?"

"Because I think I saw you in the forest."

And just as Eva said these words, a change came over the dwarf; he was the same, yet not

8

the same, and she saw that he was nothing but a huge spider, and that instead of walking on the water, as she had supposed, he had come to the boat on a web stretched across the brook, on which he was now running away just as fast as he could.

Then another of the trout put up his head, and said:

"You did well to refuse him, for if he had gotten into the boat, or if you had given him the feather, he would have put a bandage over your eyes, so that you could not see, and then would have spun a web around you and the boat, and nobody knows how you ever would have got out of it."

"He could not do it in the forest," Eva said; "how could he do it here?"

"Because first you were only brought into Shadow-Land; this time you came into it. Such as he can only control those who allow him. He could only have power over you by your own act and deed."

And once more the boat went on. But after awhile she was hailed again,—and Eva bade her stop.

This time Eva was surprised to see that the call came from a little old woman crouched upon a stone which rose above the water. A very ugly old woman she was, too; for she had a very wide mouth and a pair of prominent, staring black eyes, and she was wrapped in a green shawl, and talked in an odd little croaking voice.

"Where are you going?" she asked Eva. Eva only smiled, for she could not tell the old woman what she did not know herself.

"I know," the old woman said, nodding her head, and without waiting for a reply, "you are looking for Aster and his coat."

"How do you know?" Eva began; but the old woman interrupted her:

"Never you mind how I know it; it is enough for you that I do know it. And if you really want to find Aster, I can tell you where he is, and put you in the way of finding him."

"If you only would," Eva said, eagerly.

"You must first take me into the boat, and then give me one of your curls."

"No," Eva said, remembering what the trout had told her; "that I cannot do."

Then the old woman grew angry, and she jumped off the stone, as if she wanted to get into the boat. But as she jumped, Eva spoke to the boat, and she moved on ; and then the old woman fell into the water. And Eva saw that the old woman, changing her shape as soon as she touched the water, was nothing but the same great green frog she had seen before ; and that her shawl was the piece torn from Aster's coat which it was part of her business to find.

The third trout popped his head up out of the water :

"If you only could have known, and had given us the curl that the Green Frog asked you for, we would have made a net of it, in which we could have caught the frog, and then the hardest part of your task would have been over ; for then you could have taken the piece of Aster's coat away from her."

"If you only had told me," Eva said. "But it seems that you can only speak when it is too late."

"Because when higher powers are present we must be silent. We are never allowed to speak till after they have spoken, and are gone."

"Then, how could you have caught the frog?"

"Through the power you would have given us. But nothing can stop us or molest us now."

Then the boat went on, down the brook, and nothing more happened to stop her progress. On she went, till at last, all of a sudden, the mists and vapors before her vanished, and Eva saw, just in front of her, what seemed the open mouth of a huge serpent ready to devour them. But the boat went on until it came near the terrible jaws, and then Eva saw that they were only two great rocks, one on each side of the brook,—and the boat passed unhurt between them. And just beyond them the water stopped short; and then the boat came to a pause, and nothing that Eva could say or do would move her one inch.

And then another of the trout put up his head, and told Eva she should bid the boat go to the shore; which she did; and the boat obeyed, and then stopped again, her bow resting on the shore.

"We can do no more for you," the trout then told her. "We must now go home, for there, where the brook stops, the Enchanted River runs.

On it our boat cannot go, and in it we cannot live; so, though we would like to help you, we cannot."

Then Eva thanked them for what they had done, and taking one of her long bright curls, she tied part of it round each trout's neck, where it shone like a collar of gold. And they told her that she should keep the rest of the curl, and if at any time she was in trouble from which she could not escape, and was near water, and thought that they could help her, she should throw the rest of the curl into the water, and they would come to her.

Then, holding in her hand the two feathers the jackdaw had dropped, which the trout told her might be useful, Eva bade the trout farewell, and stepped on shore. And as her foot touched the ground, the boat moved off into the stream, and waited there.

And presently Eva said, "Go home, little boat," and the boat immediately, with the trout, began to go up the brook. She watched it till it was out of sight, and then the child stood alone on the banks of the Enchanted River.

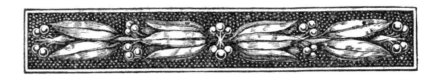

CHAPTER XIII.

THE ENCHANTED RIVER.

EVA had heard so much about this wonderful stream .that, as she stood upon its banks, she could scarcely realize that she had at last reached it. And it looked quiet enough, now that she had come to it. It had seemed to her that the waters of the Brook of Mists had ended in nothing; but now, as she stood upon the river-bank, and looked back, she could see no water. The curling mists and vapors had spread over and covered all the way by which she had come, and the only things left to show the place of the brook were the two black rocks, half hid, half revealed, by the mists playing around them. But to remain there, looking back, would, as Eva well knew, never do. Her way lay down the river, and she might as well go boldly forward. So, slowly and carefully, she began to walk along the bank.

Quiet as the river had at first seemed, it was
not very long before Eva found that it deserved
its name. What she thought was land would very
often prove to be water; and then again places
which seemed to be a broad expanse of river
would afford her a firm foothold. Here and
there were sheets of what Eva thought at first
was ice, so smooth and glassy did it look, yet
it would not be cold to the touch. The river
had no perceptible banks,—it was almost impossible to tell where earth ended and water began.
Yet, walking along, sometimes with the water
splashing above her ankles, Eva's feet were never
wet. The trees along the river seemed to walk
on, and little green flames, tipped with orange,
danced among them. Once one of these little
flames fell on Eva's dress, and when, fearing it
might burn her, she brushed it off, she found that
it was nothing but a harmless green leaf, with a
golden tip, which had dropped from a tree hanging over the river.

Many wonderful things, too, lay on the bottom
of the river. Eva saw them, and remembered
dimly what they were as she caught sight of them

through the clear water, though she could not tell where she ever had heard of them. An old lamp, rusty and cracked, she knew was Aladdin's wonderful lamp; near it lay Cinderella's little glass slippers; not far off was Blue Beard's key; and the next thing that she saw was Jack's famous bean-stalk. Seeing these things, and many more, she began to wonder if the flower which Aster had lost could possibly be among them, or if the piece of his coat was there; when she suddenly remembered that she had seen the latter in the possession of the Green Frog.

On she went, meeting no one and with no hindrance in her way. Then she saw a tiny worm, writhing, as if in pain, and trying to crawl away from a twig which lay on it and seemed to hold it. And pitying the feeble creature, even more helpless than she was, Eva stooped and took it from under the twig, and laid it gently down again. The twig immediately put forth many legs and ran away, and the worm crept into a hole near by. And a few minutes later Eva saw an old woman sitting in the water and warming her hands over a fire built upon a stone, and

L

the child went up to her, and asked her if she would tell her where Aster was. But the old woman would not even look at her; she only shook her head and mumbled something which sounded like "Ask my sister," and then she seemed, as Eva stood by her, to fall apart and melt away, and then there was nothing left of her except a little vapor, and the child saw that the fire was only a little heap of the same green leaves which she had seen among the trees.

And Eva went on, eager to leave a place where such strange things as this happened. Then the river seemed to disappear, and only a number of little pools of water were left. Picking her way carefully among them, in one she saw a poor, half-drowned mouse struggling, unable to get out ; and when Eva saw it she took the little animal in her hand and laid it on dry land. It never even looked at her, but crept shyly away, as if it was afraid of her, and hiding itself under a leaf, Eva saw it no more.

Weary and tired, the child went slowly onward. At last the pools of water were all gone, and the river flowed on as before, but its waters

were now white like milk. Tall, shadowy forms
every now and then rose from it, and made
threatening gestures ; yet they always vanished
before she came up to them. The banks of the
river became high and steep, and Eva was compelled to walk in its bed ; at times these rocky
sides were so close together that it looked as if
it would be almost impossible to pass between
them ; then again it would spread out into
a vast expanse, with no visible limit, or else the
water would run, not *down*, but *up* a rocky slope ;
it would smoke, and yet the water would be
freezingly cold ; masses of something as clear as
ice would float in this smoking water, which
were so warm that Eva could scarcely bear her
hand upon them ; on one of these masses lay a
bird, like a robin, worn and exhausted, its
feathers all wet and ruffled. Eva took it up tenderly, smoothed and dried its plumage, and held
it till it was warm. And then the bird, seemingly impatient of her gentle hold, struggled to
get free, and Eva released it, and in another moment it was gone too.

And then she came to where another old

woman sat on a rock, around which the milky
waters were foaming, and mists and vapors rose
above and behind her. To this old woman she
also spoke, and asked her the same question
which she had asked before,—where Aster was.
And in reply she was told that still farther down
the river, at the Cascade of Rocks, was where the
Toad-Woman lived, and that perhaps she might
tell Eva what it was that she wished to know.
"But," the Mist-Woman added, "my sister will
not always answer those who speak to her, and I
cannot tell you how to make her."   And, as she
spoke, the vapors thickened and gathered around
her for a moment, and then melted away, and
the Mist-Woman had vanished with them, and
nothing was left except the bare rock.

The child began to think that the wonders of
the river would never cease, and that her journey
down it would be endless.   Yet, tired as she was,
she persevered, and went on until all the water
was gone, and only stones and rocks lay in its
former bed.   But, strange to say, as Eva walked
among the stones and rocks, she found they were
only shadows.   Then, all at once, a loud noise, ·

as of falling stones, met her ear, and on coming to a sudden turn in the river, she saw that the noise was caused by what she at once knew was the Cascade of Rocks; for from a high precipice crossing the river's bed fell an endless stream of huge stones, and seated in a sort of cavern, just behind the fall, there was a third old woman, with a head like that of a toad, fanning herself with a fan made of peacock's feathers.

Eva was at first afraid to go near the woman, lest the stones should fall and crush her. But at last she ventured to go near, and she saw that at her approach the stones parted, as though to make room for her; and summoning all her courage, she went close to the cascade, and finding that none of the stones touched her, but rather got out of her way, she walked into the grotto.

The Toad-Woman stopped fanning and looked at her. Then she took a pair of spectacles out of her pocket and put them on, and Eva thought she looked funnier than ever. And then she asked :

"What do you want?"

And Eva answered, "I am looking for Aster."

" I've not got him," the old woman said.

" I know," Eva replied ; " but I was told that you might be able to tell me where he was."

"Hum !" the Toad-Woman said. " You have, then, come down the Enchanted River, and seen my sister, the Mist-Woman. But even that won't help you, though she did let you pass her, and though the stones did not trouble you. I do know where Aster is, but I promised my cousin that I would only tell it to the person who would bring me back the two feathers that her servant the jackdaw stole out of my fan."

She held up her fan as she said this, and Eva saw that two feathers out of it were gone. And then the child remembered the two feathers which the jackdaw had dropped in the boat, and which, as the trout had advised her, she had brought with her from the brook. So she showed them to the woman, and asked her if these were not the same ones which she had lost. And the Toad-Woman was very much astonished, for they were the very feathers she had been talking about.

" Take a seat," she said to Eva, " and tell me how you got them."

And then a great big brown toad hopped out of his hole when he heard his mistress say this, bringing a three-legged stool on his back. He put it down before Eva, and then went back to his hole, and Eva sat down on the stool and looked at the Toad-Woman.

"Now, tell me about it," said the Toad-Woman.

So Eva had to begin at the beginning and tell the whole story. And every time that she said anything about the green toad the old woman would nod her head, as much as to say, "I know all about that." But she never interrupted Eva; only when she was done she said to her:

" I am the only person who can help you now, and as you brought me back my feathers, I will do what I can for you. The Green Frog, who has done all this harm, is a distant cousin of mine, but she delights in doing mischief, and we have not been friends since her servant the jack-daw stole the feathers out of my fan. She it is who has got Aster, and you cannot find him until you get his coat, and the piece of it. You will have to work for them, for I cannot help you there; all I can do for you will be to send you where she lives."

Then Eva thanked the Toad-Woman very earnestly, who told her that she must be content to remain with her for that night, and the next morning that she would tell her where the Green Frog lived, and what she should do when she got there.

So that night Eva slept in the grotto behind the Cascade of Rocks. The Toad-Woman waked her up very early in the morning. She had a dress in her hand, just the color of mud, which she told Eva to put on.

"Leave your white dress here with me," she said. "Because you will have to deal with the things and the inhabitants of Shadow-Land, and it would, if it touched them, change them all into mists and shadows. Then, too, you must not be recognized."

Then the Toad-Woman tied Eva's head up in a cap, so as to hide all her golden curls, and made her wash her face and hands in some water which she gave her. Then she told her to go and look at herself in a little pool of water which was just outside of the grotto, and Eva could not help laughing when she saw herself, for face, hands, cap, and dress were all the same color.

"My cousin lives on the other side of the Cascade of Rocks," the Toad-Woman went on. "Go to her—one of my servants will show you the way—and ask her to hire you. She will not recognize you, but will take you, and will tell you that if you do your work well you may name your own wages at the end of each week. You will be able to do any work she may give you, and at the end of every week she will ask you what wages you want. Tell her you cannot say without asking your mother. Then she will tell you to go and ask her, and you must then come to me, and I will tell you what to say. In the mean time I will take care of your dress till you need it again."

Eva listened attentively to all that the Toad-Woman said to her, and thanked her for her advice. And then the woman called her servant, and the same big brown toad who had brought the stool, and who, by the way, was just the color of Eva's dress, hopped out of his hole, and his mistress bade him take Eva to where the Green Frog lived.

9

CHAPTER XIV.

THE GREEN FROG.

FOLLOWING the toad, and saying good-bye to his mistress, Eva passed unhurt through the falling stones, and picked her way carefully among those which lay in the bed of the river, till they came to the turn at which she had first caught sight of the Cascade of Rocks. There the toad hopped quickly on shore, and then he hopped across a large plain of mud, in which grew a multitude of toad-stools, and on every toad-stool, or mushroom, there sat either a frog or a toad, and in the mud at their feet were countless numbers of snakes and lizards, their long, shining bodies and tails coiled around the stalks of the toad-stools.

It was almost impossible for Eva to make any progress through the mud, over which the toad,

big as he was, hopped so lightly. Still, she suc·
ceeded in crossing the field after him, though
when they reached a firmer soil, Eva was fairly
ashamed of her dress, on which there was so much
mud ; and when they came to a little pool of clear
water, in which she saw herself reflected, she
wondered for a moment who that dirty little girl
could be ; and then she laughed to think how
very different this little mud-stained figure was
from the white-robed maiden who had passed
without a soil or a spot on her dress through the
forests of Shadow-Land.

At last they came in sight of a little hut, built
of rough stones, with a huge toad-stool for a roof,
directly in the middle of a field, which was full of
little pools of water. The field was surrounded
by a strange fence, in which the posts were all
toad-stools, and the rails all spider-webs. On
each toad-stool a green frog was sitting, and in
every web there hung either a red or a black
spider. When they came to this fence, the toad,
after going up to one of the green frogs and
croaking something to him, turned round without so much as saying "good-bye" to Eva, and

hopped away just as fast as he could go; and then one of the toad-stools, with the web attached to it, swung open as if it had been on a hinge, so that Eva could enter the inclosure.

She went up to the door of the hut and knocked. And the third time that she knocked the door was opened by a large jackdaw, which Eva immediately recognized as the same bird which she had seen on the brook, dressed in the peacock feathers which he had stolen from the Toad-Woman's fan; but although she knew him in a moment, he evidently did not know her, she was so very muddy, and so unlike her own self. In the hut, on a toad-stool, which served as a chair, sat the same Green Frog, with a little shawl over her shoulders, she had seen before, which had tried to carry Aster off, and had torn his coat; and it was with some little hesitation that Eva went up to her, and curtsied to her. And then, as she had been told, she asked the Frog if she needed a servant.

The Green Frog inspected her from head to foot.

"You are pretty dirty," she said to Eva, "and

I don't think that I ever saw you before. But that don't matter. You will have to work out-of-doors, and if you do your work properly, at the end of the week you may ask for your own wages. But if you don't work well, I will give you nothing, but I will turn you into a frog, and put you on a toad-stool, as I have done with a great many before you."

Eva thought to herself that perhaps the Frog never before had a servant like herself, so she told her that she was still willing to hire herself. Then the Frog told the jackdaw to take the new servant out and tell her what she was to do.

So the jackdaw hopped out, and Eva followed him. And when he told her what her work for that week was to be, she thought it was very funny work. And then he told her she might do as she pleased for the rest of that day, but the next morning she must go to work. And Eva amused herself by looking everywhere for Aster. But he was not to be seen. Only, just over the back-door of the hut, there hung a little wire cage, and in it there sat a little green bird, which screamed whenever the jackdaw or the Frog even

M

looked at it. And when it began to grow dark, these two took the little bird out of his cage and picked out his tail and wing-feathers, the bird screaming and struggling all the time, and then they put him back into the cage. And it was just as much afraid of Eva as it was of the jack-daw and the Frog.

There was neither sun nor moon in this place,— as in the forest, when the moon was gone, all the light seemed to come from the earth. And every morning Eva noticed that the tail and wing-feathers of the little green bird had grown again, though every evening either the Frog or the jack-daw pulled them out.

I said that when Eva was told of the work she would have to do she thought it was very queer work. Every morning, when the light drove away the darkness, she was to wipe off and dust the tops of the toad-stools on which the frogs sat, and she thought it would be very easy to do. So she tried to do it, and the jackdaw stood on one foot and cawed at her all the time,—and the more she rubbed and wiped the top of the toad-stool post the dirtier it became,—and she was nearly in

despair, when she heard one of the frogs whisper
to the other,—

"If she would only catch the jackdaw and
sweep one off with his tail, she would have no
more trouble."

And Eva did as the frog had said, and though
the jackdaw screamed and struggled, and tried to
get away, it did him no good. But she found
that when she had swept one toad-stool off that
all the rest were as clean and nice as possible,
and there was nothing more to be done to any
of them. And every evening before the Green
Frog went to sleep—she slept every night in a
little pond or pool in the corner of the hut—Eva
had to walk around the inclosure and count the
spiders and see that their webs were whole. But
she never had any trouble,—the webs were always
whole; and one of the spiders was sure to tell
her how many of them there were.

So a whole week went by, and every morning
Eva caught the jackdaw and swept one toad-stool
off with his tail. Now, Mr. Jackdaw did not at
all approve of this, and in the morning, when he
saw Eva coming, he would run away and hide

himself. Then Eva would stoop down and pre-
tend to whisper to one of the frogs; and the jackdaw, who was very inquisitive, would be so ter-
ribly afraid that something might be said that he
would like to hear, that he would come running
up in a great hurry, only to be caught and used
as a living duster.

And when the week was over Eva presented
herself to the Green Frog, and asked for her
wages. And then the old Frog asked her what
she wanted. And Eva did as the Toad-Woman
had told her, and said she would like to go and
consult her mother. This she was allowed to do,
and Eva returned, by the same road by which the
brown toad had led her, to the grotto behind the
Cascade of Rocks.

There sat the Toad-Woman, fanning herself,
just as if she had never moved since Eva first saw
her. And she knew all about the work Eva had
to do without Eva's telling her. She told Eva
to ask for the little green coat which hung at the
head of her mistress's bed (if you can call a pool
of water a bed). "She will refuse you," the
woman went on, "but you must insist. You have
earned it, and will get it in the end."

Eva thanked her, and then returned to the hut. And sitting in the door was the Frog; and she said to her that she was ready for her wages.

"What am I to give you?" croaked the Frog.

"Nothing but the little green coat which hangs at the head of your bed."

Then the Frog told her that she could not give her that, and offered her all sorts of beautiful things instead. But Eva insisted upon having the little green coat; and as fairies—even when they are bad fairies—are compelled to keep their promises or else lose their power, the Frog had to keep her word; and she told Eva that if she could find the little coat she might have it.

So Eva went into the hut and looked over the pool in which the Frog slept; and hanging against the wall were little green coats innumerable, which surprised Eva, for she never had seen anything hanging there before; and they all looked so much alike that she did not know which to choose. Then it seemed to her that a mist gathered in her eyes, and she raised her hand to rub it away, and then she saw, sitting on one of the little green coats, a beautiful, pure white moth; and then Eva saw that the other coats were only shadows, and the one on which the white moth sat was Aster's coat. So she took it down, and the moth never moved,—and then it spoke:

"Do you remember the tiny worm that you saved from the crawling twig? I was that worm; and this is the first opportunity I have had to thank you for saving my life, and the best service I could render you was this."

And without waiting to be thanked, the white moth spread her wings and was gone.

The Green Frog was angry enough when she saw that Eva had chosen rightly. But there was nothing to be done, only she grumbled to herself and said,—she did not know that Eva heard her:

"The coat is useless without the piece."

However, she hired Eva on the same terms for another week. For she thought that if the new servant failed this time she would not only change her into a frog, but get the little coat back. And the work Eva had to do this week was to empty, and then refill with fresh water every morning, the pool in which the Frog slept, and they gave her a pail with no bottom to do it with.

And Eva would have been in a sad way if she had not heard the jackdaw say, as he stood by the pool :

" Our new servant is caught at last ; for, if she did take me for a broom last week, she will never have sense enough to know that if she shakes her pail over the pool and says ' Water, go,' it will empty itself, and then ' Water, come,' and she will have no more trouble."

And then out hopped the jackdaw, and never knew that Eva heard him. And she found he was right ; and she noticed, too, that this week they only pulled out the little green bird's wing-feathers, and never touched his tail.

She did her work this time without any trouble. At the end of the week it was the same thing over again about the wages, and again Eva went to the Toad-Woman, and was told what she should do.

So she said to the Green Frog, " My coat is useless as long as it has a hole in it. You can give me the jackdaw's best cravat to mend it with."

The Frog laughed at this, and told Eva to go and get it. She did not know that the jackdaw, being fond of dress, and a thief, had stolen the piece of Aster's coat for that purpose. However, she found it out soon enough, and when Eva went to look for it,—behold! a great spider had spun a web around it,—a web so strong that she could not break it. And after trying a long time, she was nearly in despair, when she saw a little gray mouse come out of a hole, and, climbing up to the web, gnaw and bite at it with its sharp teeth till it cut it all through; and then it brought and laid in her hand the same piece of velvet which had been torn out of Aster's coat. Then the little mouse said to her:

"You saved me from being drowned, and I am not ungrateful." And then it crept back into its hole.

But when the Green Frog saw what Eva had, she was very angry, and determined to give her something which was harder to do than anything she had yet tried. So for the third week Eva's work was to wash and keep the shawl clean which the Frog wore when she went out. And the first

time that Eva tried to wash it she found that
the harder she rubbed it, and the more she tried
to clean it, the dirtier it became. `But late in
the day she heard the Green Frog say to the
jackdaw:

"I'll get my coat back, and you shall have
your cravat again, for the servant is such a dunce
that she will never learn that the only way to
clean my shawl is to lay it on a toad-stool, and
to walk around it three times, and say every
time, 'Shawl, be clean.'"

But Eva's ears were given to her for use, and,
consequently, every night the shawl was like new.
And this week she saw that they only plucked one
of the little bird's wings. The end of the week
came, and Eva, instructed by the Toad-Woman,
asked for her wages.

"What is it this time?"

"I want the little green bird that hangs in the
cage over the back-door."

"No," said the Frog, "I cannot give him to
you."

"You cannot help it," Eva said, quietly; "you
promised to pay me, and I have earned my wages.'

"Who told you anything about the little green bird," the Frog went on. "He won't sing for you, and you had better let me give you a purse full of gold."

But no, Eva would take nothing but the bird, and at last the Frog told her to go and take him, if she could find him. And then she went into the hut, grumbling and talking to herself.

Eva went to the back of the house to look for the little green bird. When she got there she did not know what to do, for there were at least fifty cages there, and in each cage was a little green bird, and cages and birds were all exactly alike,—there was no telling them apart,—and which the one she wanted could be Eva did not know. And if she chose the wrong one, all her work would be lost.

Yet, look as she might, she could not tell which was the right one. Then there was a flutter of wings in the air, and then she felt something pull her dress, and there at her feet was a beautiful bird, holding her dress in its beak, and it led her round and round the cages, and every cage that her dress touched melted away and disappeared, till there was only one cage and one bird left, and then the new bird never hesitated, but lit on the top of this cage, and then he said to Eva:

" This is Aster, who was changed by the Green Frog into this form. He cannot regain his own shape without you, and the Toad-Woman will tell you what you are to do. As soon as the Frog misses him she will know who you are, which she does not yet know, and she will do her best to get him away from you. Go at once, and without any delay, to the Cascade of Rocks. Your friend there will help you. And remember that a kind action never goes unrewarded."

And then the bird was gone, and Eva was alone. She tried to open the cage and take the little green bird out, but there was no such thing as opening it. So she took the cage, and the coat, which she had mended, and the piece had grown into the velvet, so that you never could tell that it had been torn, and without going again into the hut or telling the Frog she had found the bird, she went, for the last time, by the same road by which she had come, to the grotto of the Toad-Woman.

But she had not been gone many minutes before the Green Frog, wondering that her servant did not return to hire herself again, went in search of her. And the moment she saw that the bird was gone she knew who Eva was, and that she had discovered Aster; and, angry at herself for her own stupidity, she immediately set off in pursuit, hoping it was not yet too late to regain the prizes she had lost.

CHAPTER XV.

IN THE GROTTO.

T was with a light heart that Eva passed over the muddy way which lay between the hut and the cascade. As rapidly as she could, she went along. The little bird screamed and cried incessantly, and Eva feared, that hearing him, the frogs inhabiting this region might, by their croakings, give the alarm, and bring their powerful mistress on her track before she reached the grotto. But the frogs were all, or else seemed to be, asleep, and she passed them unnoticed.

In a very short time, which yet seemed to Eva like hours, she reached the grotto. Here she felt comparatively safe, and she would gladly have rested, but the Toad-Woman, telling her she had no time to lose, for the Green Frog knew of her escape, and that she herself was well aware of all that had happened at the hut, bade her change her dress.

Now, what Eva most wanted was to see Aster restored to his original shape. But, without a word, she obeyed the woman, and put on her own white dress again. It was so nice to get rid of that horrid, mud-colored thing she had been wearing, to shake down her long curls, instead of having them tied up in a little plain cap, and to have the ugly brown dye come off her face and hands. Eva was more than glad,—she enjoyed the change.

"Now we will help Aster," said the Toad-Woman. But the question was, how to open the cage and to get the bird out. For the cage had no door, and the bird flew round and round it, screaming and pecking at Eva's hands, till the child was nearly ready to cry. "The Frog has still power, through her enchantments, over him," the woman said. "Give me the cage, and let me see what I can do."

So she took up the cage and said some words which Eva did not understand, and then drew a circle in the air over it with her hand; and then,

"So the old woman at the head, and Eva at the tail, pulled, and pulled."

Page 147.

to Eva's great amazement, a door in the cage opened and the woman put her hand in it and took out the bird, which screamed louder and pecked harder than ever.

"Now," said the Toad-Woman, "we must make all the haste we can. We must find Aster before the Frog gets here. I'll hold the bird's head, and you take his tail, and then pull,—pull as hard as you can."

All this was so queer to Eva, who thought they had found Aster, that she could not understand it. But the old woman saw her trouble, and, without getting angry or impatient, as some fairies would have done, she said to Eva:

"Aster is sewed up in the bird's skin. And we can only get him out by tearing it apart. Make haste, there is no time to be lost."

So the old woman at the head, and Eva at the tail, pulled, and pulled, and pulled. And the harder they pulled, the more the bird screamed and cried, till Eva pitied him so that she could scarcely bear to hurt him. But whenever she would want to stop the Toad-Woman would tell her to pull harder.

Such a tough skin as it was, to be sure !   There seemed to be no such thing as tearing it, and the Toad-Woman said that Aster must have been very naughty before he fell into the Green Frog's hands.   And Eva, much as she loved Aster, could not contradict this.

But at last the bird left off screaming, and hung between them as if it was dead.   And then, as the two pulled, it got larger and longer, and the feathers were farther apart, and then all of a sudden the skin gave way and vanished, where, Eva did not know, and from it there dropped, just in time for Eva to save it from falling to the floor of the grotto, Aster's tiny figure, motionless, and as it were, asleep, and just like what he had been when Eva first received him, except that his coat was in her hands; and the Toad-Woman had only time enough to tell her to put it on him, and Eva had just obeyed, and was stooping to kiss the little prince as he lay in her lap, when they heard a loud croak, and with a long leap the Green Frog was in the grotto.

But as soon as she saw Eva, standing there in her spotless white robe, holding the unconscious

little prince, she knew how it was that he had
been taken from her, and that her power over
him was nearly gone. Yet she knew that if she
could once again obtain possession of him that
no one could rescue him; and as Eva had once
submitted to her, she had no power of herself,
as she before possessed, to protect him. And
without even looking at the Toad-Woman, she
was going to leap upon Aster, and try and snatch
him from Eva's arms, when the Toad-Woman,
taking from her pocket a curl, which even in that
moment Eva recognized as part of the one which
she had cut to give to the trout, and which had
lain, forgotten ever since, in the pocket of her
own white dress, dropped it on the ground. And
as the hair touched the ground a spring of clear
water came bubbling up, and in it Eva saw her
friends, the six trout, whom she recognized by
the golden collars they wore; and the Green Frog
was so surprised that she stopped to look, and
then the water covered her, and before she could
move, the trout, as they had once said they could,
do, swam up to her and enveloped her in a net
made of these golden hairs, which the Frog could

not break, and then, in spite of all her efforts to escape, and her loud croakings, the floor of the grotto opened, and spring, trout, and Frog were gone in a moment.

It all passed in less time than can be told, and once more Eva and the Toad-Woman were alone.

"Your hardest work is over," the woman said to her. "The three tasks are done ; you have found Aster, his coat, and its piece. Here you cannot stay any longer. When the moon is full again Aster's long-lost flower will bloom, and you will find it."

And then a sudden darkness came over everything, and when, a moment later, the light returned, nothing was as it had been. The Toad-Woman, her grotto, and the Cascade of Rocks were gone, and when Eva heard the music which heralded the coming of the moon, and saw the silver crescent rise to its place, and Aster once more woke from his sleep, she could scarcely realize that she was again in the old, familiar forest, and the past seemed like a dream.

For in that moment of darkness, the Enchanted River had disappeared, and Eva knew that the search in truth was nearly over.

CHAPTER XVI.

ASTER'S STORY.

ONCE more Eva and Aster, hand in hand, wandered, as they both had feared they would never again be allowed to do, through the forest, by the light of the fair young moon, which looked down upon them from the sky. And nothing came now to disturb them; no hideous faces mocked at them from behind shrub or tree; no hostile beings, in shape of spider or of frog, strove to take Aster from his young guardian. Nor were they limited, as before, to the narrow path which had previously confined their steps; but they might wander, unmolested, as their fancy led them, through the forest. Shadows still surrounded them, yet these shadows were fair and lovely to look upon : groups of sweet child-figures at play, or fair faces which smiled on the two as they passed.

Flowers, too, more brilliant and beautiful in hue than any they had yet found, bloomed wherever they looked. Not the pale, scentless blossoms they had seen before, but flowers which greeted them with rich perfume, and whose bells and chalice-like cups, touched lightly by the dress of the children as they passed, rang forth in bright and joyous melody. In the bells of the flowers sat and swung tiny and beautiful shapes, which Aster told Eva were the Flower Fairies, the gentlest of the race, whose sole duty was to carry perfume to, and color the flowers. Some bathed in the dewdrops on the leaves, others rode, seated on beautiful butterflies, but all seemed gay and happy.

The light shed by the growing crescent of the moon seemed brighter; the soft music which hailed her coming more joyous and triumphant; the clouds, reflecting the moon's light, wore a rich, rosy tint, reminding Eva of the light in the Valley of Rest; the grass was green, and soft as velvet,—the little sparkling brooks which they occasionally crossed all sung the same song:

> When will Eva's task be done?
> When will Aster's flow'r be won?
> When his robes from stains are free,—
> When the moon's orb round shall be,—
> Then the trial will be done,
> Then shall Aster's flow'r be won.

For a few days, however, Eva noticed that Aster seemed dull and spiritless. He scarcely ever spoke, but walked quietly by her side. Nothing seemed to attract his attention, nothing made him smile; but every now and then, when they would cross one of the little brooks, and it would sing its song, he would look down upon his dress, and say, sadly:

" It will never be bright again!"

Yet Eva noticed that he was careful never to trample on the flowers, or to hurt anything in their path. And as, day after day, the moon brightened and broadened, and Aster grew with her increase, Eva saw that the sad, mournful expression in his eyes vanished, and they regained their former starlike brilliancy. By slow degrees the spots and the stains upon his dress disappeared ; and, as they faded away, Aster became once more his own playful and happy self. Never before had he been as gentle or as docile and affectionate as he now was, though he was very silent ; and Eva thought, could he only be always as he was now she would be content never to leave him ; and she began to think, almost with dread, of their approaching separation.

On and on they went, till they came to a place where a tiny spring, bright as a living diamond, gushed up joyously, singing to itself for very gladness. Soft green mosses and pure white flowers grew around it ; and when Aster saw it, he sprang forward with a joyous cry, and seating himself near it, he beckoned to Eva to follow his example.

Then, for the first time since the two had been together, for he had never before mentioned the past, so that Eva almost thought he had forgotten it, Aster asked her to tell him how she ever had found him again.

And once more Eva told the story,—this time to an interested listener,—how, after she missed

him, she had sought him, but in vain, among the
marked holes, and, seeking him, had climbed the
rock to the door of the Valley of Rest; how she
had been admitted, and had dwelt among the
Happy Children till, the day of their absence,
the little brook had brought her the piteous cry,
"Eva! Eva! help me!" How this cry had recalled all she had forgotten, how the Dawn Fairies
had given her the magic boat, in which she had
gone through the cavern and down the Brook of
Mists,—and then, leaving the boat, had gone, all
alone, up the Enchanted River to the grotto of
the Toad-Woman behind the Cascade of Rocks;
how the woman had advised her, and how she
had served the Green Frog; what the moth, the
mouse, and the bird had done for her; how the
skin covering the little green bird had been torn;
and how, after the Frog was carried away by
the friendly Fish Fairies, she had known that the
worst was over, and the search nearly done.

Aster listened, and when Eva paused, he began; and it seemed to her that, as he told his
story, he spoke as he had never before spoken,—
as if he was older, and more matured.

"I can tell you now," he said, "now that it is all nearly over, who THEY were of whom you used to wonder that I spoke. The Green Frog and her servants were the visible forms of THEY to whom my punishment was committed. Yet, had I obeyed you,—which was part of my trial,—you, under whose care my friends, who advised you in the shape of the toad and the Toad-Woman, were allowed to place me, but little of this trouble would have come upon me. If I failed in obedience to you,—such was the condition,—if THEY gained the slightest hold upon me,—I must fall wholly into their power, and then only, if you really wished it, could your Love have power to overcome their Hate. And you know, Eva, how I fell into their hands."

"Yes, I know," Eva said; "but I do not yet see why you crept into the crevice in the rock."

"How could I help it?" Aster asked. "After all I had done, and all that had happened before! Because what must be, will be, and THEY made me."

"And then, after you went into the rock?" Eva asked, eagerly. "Remember, I know nothing of that."

Then Aster told her how, in the crevice of the rock, he had found that the Green Frog lay in wait for him. How she and her servants had taken him, bound and tied with the same spider's web from which Eva had, once before, in the forest, released him, to her hut in the field of mud. And how, when there, he had to lie in the mud, as a footstool for the Frog,—and that every night she made him stand before her, and would laugh at him, and ask him why Eva and his friends did not come to help him.

"I was too proud," Aster said, "and too angry, to call for you. I thought I·should, by myself, be able to escape. I tried, but the power of THEY who kept me was too great for me, and I never once succeeded even in passing the strange fence around the hut.

"But all the time, Eva, I knew—and it was part of my punishment—that an appeal to you could be heard,·and that you would come to help me. But that I—I, a prince,—powerful at home, and only weak now because I had lost such a trifling thing as a flower, should be compelled to ask help of one who was able to help me only because

O

she was gentler and kinder than I was,—I could not do it. Meantime, the Green Frog laughed at my efforts to escape. Yet, do what she would to me, I never called for you. She might hang me up in the spider's web,—she might threaten to crush me,—I was silent.

"At last I could stand it no longer. I must help to carry heavy stones, and when their weight nearly crushed me,—for though only shadows to you, they were realities to me,—I would have rested, the spider would sting me and scorch me with his poisonous breath,—the jackdaw peck me, —and the Green Frog would threaten to swallow me, and tell me that now you never would come to me, for the Dawn Fairies had made you forget me. And not till then, when they told me you had forgotten me, did I speak; and the only words that I said were these, 'Eva! Eva! help me!'"

"Yes," Eva said, "those are the same words that the brook brought me." And then she told Aster about her dream: how the faces had asked why he lost his flower; and the frog had spoken of his coat; and the spider asked why he crept into the rock ; and how, between it all, had come the wailing cry of "Eva! Eva! help me!"

Then, too, Aster told her how they had spoken of what she must do, and that they thought she never would do it, or know what was to be done. And then he went on :

" But at last the Green Frog grew angry, when she found that, no matter what she said or did, I only answered, 'Eva! Eva! help me!' For then, making her servants strip off my coat, she touched me with a stick, and said to me :

" 'You shall never let Eva hear you. I will silence you.'

" And, as she spoke, I was changed all at once into the little green bird in whose shape you found me. And then the Frog, putting me in a cage, said :

" 'You can never get out till your friend gets the piece of your coat, the coat itself, and then finds you. If she does these things, you may be free ; but these things she cannot do unless others help her ; and not till after all these things are done can she hope to find your flower again.'

" The rest, Eva, you know."

As Aster spoke, Eva looked at him. And she saw that, on the rich, green velvet of his dress, only a few tiny spots and stains were left; and then she began to wonder what would happen when the moon would again be full, and the flower they had sought so long should bloom and be found. Would Aster then return to his home? and, as for herself, what would become of her?

But she did not wonder long, for the soft music which attended the disappearance of the moon thrilled through the forest, and Eva and Aster, by the side of the spring, lay down and slept. And, once more, as on the first night that Eva, holding the tiny form of Aster to her heart, had slept on the mossy bed where once the golden fountain had played, the two fair white forms bent over the sleeping children, and one said:

"The punishment is over."

"Yes," was the other's reply, "Love has overcome Hate, and Aster has been led back, through its gentle influences, to his true self once more."

Yet, even as they spoke, two figures, with the hateful faces Eva had seen, crept slowly up through the darkness to where the children lay. But the white forms, hovering over their sleep, spoke :

"Go back, oh, evil fairies! to the dark shadows among which ye dwell! Here your power is over, and our Prince is a prince once more."

And, with a low cry of disappointment and rage, the two, turning away from the bright forms, shrank into the darkness, and were seen no more. Then, with a smile on their beautiful faces, the two bright forms bent caressingly over the sleepers; and a moment later they, too, were gone, and Eva and Aster were alone.

CHAPTER XVII.

THE LAST OF SHADOW-LAND.

ONCE again there rang through the forest a strain of rich and gleeful music. Once more the moon rose, a bright, unbroken circle, to her station in the sky. A soft, rosy light lingered everywhere; flowers of rarer beauty than ever, bloomed in profusion; the murmur of the spring was sweeter than ever, and as Eva awoke, and looked at Aster, she saw that neither spot nor stain defaced his rich dress, but that it was as unsullied as her own. And as she looked upon her young companion, now as tall as herself, and with something in his bearing Eva had never been conscious of before,—something noble and princelike,—she heard a voice from the spring murmuring, in soft, melodious tones:

(162)

" 'Tis the hour!
Aster's flower
Here shall bloom!"

And oh! what a sweet smile curved Aster's lips as he heard these words! Yet, when Eva would have spoken, he laid his hand gently upon her mouth, as though to command silence; and the child, feeling that their positions, somehow, were strangely reversed,—that it was now Aster's turn to command and hers to obey,—was silent.

The two stood, looking into the clear water of the spring. Then Aster seated himself on the moss, in silence, and beckoned to Eva to do the same, and without hesitating she followed his example.

They sat, not a word passing between them, and on each fair face was a different expression. On Aster's was all joyous expectation, all smiles and happiness; on Eva's there was a serious look, almost amounting to mournfulness. It pained her, more than she was willing to confess, to think that, after all she had borne and done for Aster, he should welcome their separation so gladly; for, however much they might wish to remain together, the finding of the flower would be the signal for their parting; and the toil and trouble through which Eva had passed for Aster's sake had only the more endeared him to her. He seemed already far, far away from her, and Eva knew she was no longer necessary to him.

And as Eva, sitting by Aster's side, thought of all this, somehow the place where they sat seemed to grow more familiar; another and a well-known sound mingled with the other sounds of the forest,—the voice of falling waters. And then, as Aster's face grew brighter and more expectant, and his starlike eyes sparkled, Eva felt a sudden dimness gather in her own, and first one large tear and then another rolled down her cheeks, and dropped, as she bent over it, into the waters of the little spring.

But she was wholly unprepared for what followed. Aster sprang to his feet, and the words, "Look, Eva, look!" passed his lips. And as Eva, her hand now clasped in his, looked, the spring bubbled and foamed, and then, its waters parting, up rose from its bosom the Golden

Fountain, with its clouds of glistening, golden spray; its rainbow sparkles of colored light; its musical fall, and its dancing elves, as she had long since seen it.

Nor was this all. For, even as the children gazed, there appeared in the calm water at the foot of the fountain a bud, folded in soft, green leaves; and, by slow degrees, as Eva looked, the bud rose from the encircling foliage, and its stem grew higher and higher, and then, slowly and gracefully, its pure white petals opened, like a fair and stainless ivory cup enfolding a golden torch, and it breathed forth the fragrance of many violets: and, as Eva looked, she knew that the search was over, and the pure white lily before them was Aster's flower, won at last.

Then Eva's blue eyes shone with joy, and her fair cheeks flushed, and she turned to Aster:

"Aster, be glad; for your flower is won, and all that remains is for you to pluck it."

"No," he said, slowly; "that is not for me to do. I can only receive it as your gift, Eva; I am not worthy to gather it,—that can only be done by your hand."

And Eva, bending over the water, plucked the beautiful lily, with its long stem, and laid it in Aster's hand. And, as his fingers clasped the gift, a swell of music thrilled through the air, and Eva saw, hovering over them, the two fair, white forms which had come before, and which she at once knew had, under the shapes of the toad and the Toad-Woman, led and advised her, and she pointed them out to Aster. And, as Aster raised his eyes to them, they beckoned to him, and smiled upon Eva; and she knew that all was over, and the moment had come for them to part.

Still, not a word passed between them. Eva's eyes were fixed upon Aster,—his were raised to the bright hovering forms. Then, holding the lily in his hand, he turned to Eva and pressed his lips to her brow.

"That was the kiss with which you woke me, Eva, given back to you,—this is because I love you."

He kissed her lips, and as he did so a bright crimson light flashed suddenly around them, dazzling Eva's blue eyes, so that she involuntarily closed them, and then the sweet breath of violets floated around them, and all was still.

———

Eva sat up, and rubbed her eyes. Tall, wavy grass grew all around her, violets, dandelions, and buttercups bloomed through it, and her lap was full of the pretty field-flowers. Bees were buzzing and collecting honey,—butterflies floated lazily about on their black-and-golden wings,—the brown beetle, with his long black feelers, swung on the tall grass-stalk,—the crickets chirped,— the snail had put out his horns,—the old mill-pond glistened and shone in the long, slanting rays of the setting sun,—there was her father's house, — everything was just as it used to be, except the green toad, and that was a very important exception.

And while Eva was rubbing her eyes, and trying to think where she could be, and what all this meant, she heard the tea-bell ring, and as that was very easy to understand, she got up and went to the house. She peeped through the window before she went in, and everything seemed right in there.   For her mother was just folding up her work,—the baby was crowing and playing with his rattle in the cradle,—strawberries and cream and sponge-cake were on the table; and when Eva came quietly in, and slipped into her seat by her father, he put his hand on her curls, and asked her if she had had a nice time down by the pond the whole afternoon.

"Yes, papa," was all Eva could say, and then she paid very strict attention to her saucer of ripe strawberries covered with cream.

Presently her mother said:

"My little girl had a nice long nap this afternoon.   I called her once, and she only raised her head for a minute, and then down it went again."

Papa laughed.

"Strawberries and cream waked her up at last."

And Eva never said a word.

But to this day she never sees a shooting-star without wondering what has been lost in the moon,—she never sees a toad without thinking it may be a fairy in disguise, and every lily re-calls Aster and his flower.

For Eva believes in fairies. Why should she not? She knows all about them. She has never told any one,—not even papa, though he never laughs at her; but if Eva should live to be an old woman—and I hope she may!—she will never forget her

ADVENTURES IN SHADOW-LAND.

P

JUVENILE PUBLICATIONS

OF

J. B. LIPPINCOTT & CO.,

PHILADELPHIA.

———◦◦◦———

For sale by all Booksellers, or will be sent by mail, postage free, on receipt of price.

———◦◦◦———

ARTHUR'S ALL'S FOR THE BEST SERIES. In handsome box, containing: All's for the best; Heroes of the Household; The Seen and the Unseen. By T. S. ARTHUR. 3 vols. 16mo. Illustrated. Extra cloth. $2.25.

ARTHUR'S NEW JUVENILE LIBRARY. In box, containing: Who is Greatest? The Poor Wood-Cutter; Mr. Haven't-Got-Time; The Wounded Boy; Uncle Ben's New-Year's Gift; Pierre, the Organ-Boy; Who are Happiest? Maggie's Baby; The Peacemakers; The Lost Children; Our Harry; The Last Penny. By T. S. ARTHUR. 12 vols. With seventy-two Illustrations. Cloth, gilt back. $7.50.

BOYS' GLOBE LIBRARY. (FIRST SERIES.) In handsome box, containing: Sandford and Merton; Robinson Crusoe; The Arabian Nights' Entertainments; The Swiss Family Robinson. 4 vols. 12mo. Each with six Steel Plates printed in colors. Extra cloth. $6.00.

BOYS' GLOBE LIBRARY. (SECOND SERIES.) In handsome box, containing: Pictures of Heroes, and Lessons from their Lives; Forty-four Years of a Hunter's Life; Fighting the Flames; Old Deccan Days, or Hindoo Fairy Legends. 4 vols. 12mo. With numerous Illustrations. Extra cloth. $6.00.

CHAMBERS'S LIBRARY FOR YOUNG PEO-PLE. (FIRST SERIES.) In box, containing: Alfred in India; Duty and Affection; Fireside Amusements; Grandmamma's Pocket; Moral Courage; Old England, a Tale; History of Scotland; Swan's Egg; Truth and Trust; Self-Denial; Clever Boys, and other Stories; History of England; History of France; Little Robinson; Orlandino; Poems for Young People; Steadfast Gabriel, a Tale; True Heroism, and other Stories; Uncle Sam's Money-Box; The Whisperer. 20 vols. 16mo. With twenty Engravings on Steel. Extra cloth, gilt back. $10.00.

CHAMBERS'S LIBRARY FOR YOUNG PEO-PLE. (SECOND SERIES.) In box, containing: Alice Errol, and other Tales; My Birthday Book; Tales and Songs for Young Singers; Midsummer at Hay Lodge; Voices of Spring Flowers; Little Museum-Keepers; Wild Flowers and their Uses. 7 vols. 16mo. With seven Illustrations. Extra cloth, gilt back. $3.50.

CAMEOS FROM ENGLISH HISTORY. From Rollo to Edward II. By the author of " The Heir of Redclyffe." With Marginal Index. 12mo. Tinted paper. Cloth. $1.25. Extra cloth. $1.75.

" History is presented in a very attractive and interesting form for young folks in this work."—*Pittsburg Gazette.*
" An excellent design happily executed."—*N. Y. Times.*

CAST UP BY THE SEA. A book for Boys from Eight Years Old to Eighty. By Sir SAMUEL W. BAKER, author of " The Albert N'Yanza," etc. With ten Illustrations by Huard, and Vignette Title. 12mo. Toned paper. Cloth. 75 cents. Fine edition. Extra cloth. $1.25.

CASELLA; or, The Children of the Valleys.

By MARTHA FARQUHARSON, author of "Elsie Dinsmore," etc. 16mo. Cloth. $1.50.

"A lively and interesting story, based upon the sufferings of the pious Waldenses, and is well written and life-like."—*Boston Chr. Era.*

"It is rich in all that is strong, generous, and true."—*Baltimore Episc. Methodist.*

"The story is one of the most interesting in ecclesiastical History."—*The Methodist.*

DEEP DOWN. A Tale of the Cornish Mines.

By R. M. BALLANTYNE, author of "Fighting the Flames," "Silver Lake," etc. With Illustrations. *Globe Edition.* 12mo. Fine cloth. $1.50

"'Deep Down' can be recommended as a story of exciting interest, which boys will eagerly read, and which will give some valuable ideas on a subject about which very little is generally known. The book is embellished with a number of very excellent designs."—*Phila. Ev. Telegraph.*

"The author, through the attractive medium of a well-told story, has managed to give a vast amount of valuable information within a limited space."—*N. Y. Ev. Mail.*

ELSIE MAGOON; or, The Old Still-House. A

Temperance Tale. Founded upon the actual experience of every-day life. By MRS. FRANCES D. GAGE. 12mo. Cloth. $1.50.

ERLING THE BOLD. A Tale of the Norse

Sea-Kings. By R. M. BALLANTYNE, author of "Fighting the Flames," "Deep Down," etc. *Globe Edition.* With Illustrations. 12mo. Extra cloth. $1.50.

FEW FRIENDS (A), And How They Amused

Themselves. A Tale in Nine Chapters, containing Descriptions of Twenty Pastimes and Games, and a Fancy-Dress Party. By MARY E. DODGE, author of "Hans Brinker," etc. 12mo. Extra cloth. $1.25.

"In the name of many readers, seniors as well as juniors, we thank Mrs. Dodge for a very pleasant and fascinating volume, which cannot fail to be in great demand during the holidays."—*Phila. Press.*

"It is not only useful but entertaining, and just the thing for holiday parties."—*Boston Advertiser.*

FIGHTING THE FLAMES. A Tale of the London Fire Brigade. By R. M. BALLANTYNE, author of "Silver Lake," "The Coral Islands," etc. With Illustrations. *Globe Edition*. 12mo. Fine cloth. $1.50.

"An interesting and spirited little work."—*Phila. Ev. Telegraph.*

FORTY-FOUR YEARS OF A HUNTER'S LIFE. Being Reminiscences of Meshach Browning, a Maryland Hunter. With numerous Illustrations. *Globe Edition*. 12mo. Fine cloth. $1.50.

"It is a book which will be read with the greatest avidity by thousands in all sections of the country; and we rejoice in the belief that the worthy old hunter will be cheered, before he closes his earthly career, with a substantial recompense."—*Baltimore American.*

FUZ-BUZ AND MOTHER GRABEM. The Wonderful Stories of Fuz-Buz the Fly and Mother Grabem the Spider. A Fairy Tale. Handsomely illustrated. Small 4to. Cloth. $1.00. Extra cloth, gilt top. $1.25.

"Laughable stories, comically illustrated for little folks. The very book to delight little boys and girls. Get it for the holidays."—*Pittsburg Chronicle.*

LITTLE ONES' LIBRARY. In box, containing: A Gift for the Little Ones at Home; Nursery Songs and Rhymes; The Lily; Little Pet's Book; The Dew-Drop; The Faithful Dog; Grandfather's Visit; The Pet Lamb; Songs and Stories; The Widow's Cottage; The Pet Squirrel; The Home Story Book. With numerous Illustrations. 12 vols. 18mo. Cloth, gilt back. $4.00. Paper covers. $1.60.

QUAKER PARTISANS (THE). An exciting Story of the Revolution. By the author of "The Scout." With Illustrations. 12mo. Fine cloth. $1.50.

"It is a story of stirring incidents turning upon the actual movements of the war, and is told in an animated style of narrative which is very attractive. Its handsome illustrations will still further recommend it to the young people."—*New York Times.*

MAN UPON THE SEA; or, A History of Maritime Adventure, Exploration, and Discovery, from the Earliest Ages to the Present Time. With numerous Engravings. By FRANK B. GOODRICH, author of "The Court of Napoleon," etc. 8vo. Cloth. $2.25.

"This eloquent and well-illustrated volume contains a large amount of rare and interesting information, conveyed in an easy and very pleasant style."—*Boston Recorder.*

"By its judicious selection of topics, its skillful condensation, and its agreeable style, it is adapted to supply the place in the library of no small number of voluminous and costly works."—*New York Tribune.*

"The book will be warmly welcomed by young people."—*Boston Post.*

OLD DECCAN DAYS; or, Hindoo Fairy Legends current in Southern India. Collected from oral tradition by M. FRERE. With an Introduction and Notes by Sir BARTLE FRERE. *Globe Edition.* 12mo. Illustrated. Fine cloth. $1.50.

"This little collection of Hindoo Fairy Legends is probably the most interesting book extant on that subject. * * * The stories of this little book are told in a very lively and agreeable style,—a style few writers of English possess, but which, when it belongs to a lady, is the best and most attractive in the world."—*N. Y. Times.*

OUR OWN BIRDS; or, A Familiar Natural History of the Birds of the United States. By WILLIAM L. BAILY. Revised and Edited by EDWARD D. COPE, Member of the Academy of Natural Sciences. With full Index. With numerous Illustrations. 16mo. Toned paper. Extra cloth. $1.50.

"To the youthful, 'Our Own Birds' is likely to prove a bountiful source of pleasure, and cannot fail to make them thoroughly acquainted with the birds of the United States. As a science there is none more agreeable to study than ornithology. We therefore feel no hesitation in commending this book to the public. It is neatly printed and bound, and is profusely illustrated."—*New York Herald.*

RIFLE AND HOUND IN CEYLON. Hunting Adventures in Ceylon. By Sir SAMUEL W. BAKER, author of "Cast Up by the Sea," etc. With Illustrations. 12mo. Fine cloth. $1.50.

SILVER LAKE; or, Lost in the Snow. By R. M. BALLANTYNE, author of "The Wild Man of the West," "Fighting the Flames," etc. With Illustrations. Square 12mo. Tinted paper. Extra cloth. $1.25.

"We heartily recommend the book, and can imagine the pleasure many a young heart will receive on its perusal."—*The Eclectic Review.*

TALKS WITH A CHILD. Talks with a Child on the Beatitudes. Second edition. 18mo. Extra cloth. 75 cents. Flexible cloth. 50 cents.

"A volume written in a sweet, devout, simple, and tender spirit, and calculated to edify the old as well as the young."—*Boston Ev. Trans.*

TREES, PLANTS, AND FLOWERS: Where, and How they Grow. By WILLIAM L. BAILY, author of "Our Own Birds," etc. With seventy-three Engravings. 16mo. Toned paper. Extra cloth.

TUTOR'S COUNSEL (A). En Avant, Messieurs! Being a Tutor's Counsel to his Pupils. By the Rev. G. H. D. MATHIAS, M.A. 16mo. Fine cloth. $1.50.

"Every page of the book contains matter that will profit not only the young, but the old."—*Boston Com'l Bulletin.*

CPSIA information can be obtained at www.ICGtesting.com
Printed in the USA
BVOW02s1026180614

356728BV00008B/276/P

9 781246 107340